D1384357

We're Doing CX Wrong... And How To Get It Right

Nicholas Zeisler, CCXP

ISBN: 978-0-578-97503-0

DEDICATION

For Jared, Amanda, Mina, Bonita, Kevin, Dave, and Marilu:
The Original CX Dream Team

CONTENTS

ACKNOWLEDGMENTS

Thanks to Mark Tamer, Bill LaSalle, Larry Roush, John Henderson, Barry Pollard, and Amy Shore for their reading of and thoughts on my drafts.

*

Thanks to Marjorie Hook and Rex Tibbens for their years-long mentorship.

*

Thanks to Dan Gingiss, Nate Brown, Nick Glimsdahl, Jeremy Watkin, Neal Topf, Paul Catherall, Ben Goodey, Gavin Scott, James Dodkins, and Rick Denton for their thought leadership in CX (especially when we disagree).

*

And thanks most of all to Ron Miletta for his patience in this endeavor, and so many others over the years.

FOREWORD:

"Hey, I've got an idea," said the insidious Finance Guy at an airline years ago (I don't know why, but I'm pretty sure it was a guy). "Let's start charging passengers to check their bags!"

"But that's always been a service we've included in the ticket price," said his far-more-rational peer.

"Who cares? We have to keep ticket prices low to be competitive, so let's add this fee separately and then we can still advertise low ticket prices!"

So began the long, dark journey airlines took to find as many different fees as possible to tack on to their "low" ticket prices. And it made them billions and billions of dollars. One airline even considered—but eventually abandoned—the idea of charging to use the plane's restrooms.

It's not like the airline industry was the first to think of this. Have you bought a ticket to a sporting event or theater production lately? The additional fees, one of them ironically termed a "*convenience fee*," can often tack on 30-40% to the ticket price. And don't get me started on the "resort fees" in places like Las Vegas, the daily charges of $35 or more for mandatory "conveniences" like the fitness center that used to be free.

These are business decisions that are made without any thought given to Customer experience. And, not surprisingly, they often result in very unhappy Customers.

In other words, it is how companies are doing Customer Experience (CX) wrong.

They're focused entirely on the bottom line without regard to the impact such decisions make on the very people that fund Finance Guy's salary—their Customers.

Those Customers now have far more choices than at any time in history, a (loud) voice on social media, and a simple yet critical desire—to be treated like more than an account number (or frequent flier number) by the companies with which they spend their hard-earned dollars.

These same companies are trying; really they are. They're collecting lots of survey data and telling all of their Customers that their "feedback is very important to us." They're calculating Net Promotor Scores and Customer Satisfaction Scores and even things like Customer Effort Scores.

They're putting all of these important scores into a weekly or monthly report and sharing that report with management, along with high fives and congratulations when the scores go up (and excuses or rationalizations when they go down).

You know what most companies are *not* doing? Actually talking with their Customers. Like face-to-face or telephone or even Zoom talking. They're not heeding the advice of countless CX professionals and stepping into the shoes of their Customers by literally becoming a Customer and observing how difficult everything is when it should be simple.

They're reporting all of these scores without any context whatsoever. They know *HOW* the company is doing, but not *WHY*. And if they don't know why, how can they take action? How can they do more of what they're doing well and less of what annoys their Customers?

The answer is they can't.

Until now.

With his smart, funny, accessible, and utterly relevant new book, *We're Doing CX Wrong…And How To Get It Right*, Nicholas Zeisler calls out the bad and the ugly, and highlights the good.

More than once you're going to read about "doing CX wrong" and think, *Darn it, that's exactly what we're doing.* But be patient, for Nicholas will lead you to the promised land of CX with all the ways to do CX *right*.

With military precision, he pulls back the curtain on CX philosophies and operational maneuvers that just don't make any sense, and then outlines a simple and practical plan for getting CX right.

So, if every CEO of every company would just read Nicholas' book, we might get rid of checked bag fees and convenience fees and resort fees for good.

-Dan Gingiss

Author of *The Experience Maker: How To Create Remarkable Experiences That Your Customers Can't Wait To Share*

INTRODUCTION

Say an alien lands on Earth and avails himself of some of our human goods and services. Shortly afterwards, he receives the *typical* Net Promoter System (NPS) survey invitation with the *typical*, "How likely are you to recommend Acme, Inc., products to your friends, relatives, or co-workers?" question. Not being from here, and all of his friends, relatives, and co-workers residing back on his home planet lightyears away, unlikely ever to find themselves in a position to buy Acme, Inc., products, he may scratch his head with one of his tentacles wondering about the question. After all, he's here to observe us and learn about our customs. This question seems ponderous to him.

Now, perhaps he's an alien with an MBA, so he considers the potential business utility of the question: Maybe this is part of Acme's marketing plan that's built mostly on word-of-mouth (or word-of-whatever organ aliens use to communicate with each other). But he knows Acme does a *lot* of traditional marketing and advertising and is a very well-known brand already. Try as hard as he can, he can't come to any sort of understanding as to why Acme asked him this question, especially on a survey that's so obviously about his most recent experience with the brand and how he did or didn't enjoy it. The question itself seems a bit too spot-on. What on earth (literally), are they trying to glean from the responses?

If the alien were to come across Fred Reichheld, the inventor of NPS, or just about any other modern human Customer Experience practitioner, he'd receive a lecture on the use and wonderful value of

NPS, how its score is calculated, and how adept it is at predicting business outcomes like sales, revenue, and market share. That only makes matters more confusing to him. "So," the alien might ask, "by asking your Customers how likely they are to recommend your products or services to others, you can predict how your future sales and revenue will perform? That seems a bit clever. Perhaps too much. Besides, the arithmetical foundation of this particular formula is pretty sketchy—one oughtn't simply subtract *percentages*[1] from each other like that. And to use the resulting calculation in a predictive model? Woo boy! *Our* species would never have mastered intergalactic travel if we'd been so cavalier about mathematics. No wonder you haven't even gotten a person to Mars yet. By the way, the CX there is terrible...it's all bots."

A spirited argument may ensue, but surely any earthly CX expert would be gracious, wise, and friendly enough to avoid causing an intergalactic scene over NPS scores. Still, it's unlikely that either side would end up convincing the other. Somehow, however, businesses and their leaders here on Earth have persuaded themselves of the efficacy of NPS, even though the mathematics don't really hold up to scrutiny and the logic itself is contrived and more than a bit convoluted. For that matter, this isn't just to pick on NPS, C-SAT, Customer Effort Score, or any other metric per se. As we'll discover, the formulation of any particular KPI isn't even the biggest issue with how we measure our CX performance.

With this book, I intend to highlight a few ways, like this, in which we're getting CX wrong. I plan to untangle the logic so we can explore how we can get it right; and with a more logical approach and a proven framework, I will demonstrate how to implement CX as a function in your company or organization. It's not geared toward aliens, *explicitly*;

---

[1] In the NPS scoring formulation, the Likelihood to Recommend responses (on a 0-10 scale) are categorized as either "Detractors" (those responding 0-6), "Neutrals" (7s and 8s), or "Promoters" (9s and 10s). The percentage of Detractors is subtracted from the percentage of Promoters. By "subtracted from," I mean that percentages are stripped (i.e., 45% Promoters simply becomes "45," while 15% Detractors becomes "15"), and the corresponding difference in those whole numbers is the Net Promoter Score (here it'd be +30). I know, I know. As a mathematician and statistician, when I first saw this egregious formulation, I was taken aback.

This is a book for business leaders who generally appreciate the basic goal of prioritizing and driving efforts for the benefit of their Customers' experiences, and are looking for practical and straight-forward ways to "*do* CX" in their organizations.

If you're looking for a justification of CX ("What's the ROI?"), you won't find it here. Rather, the target audience is CEOs and business leaders who already *conceive* of the value of Customer Experience as an endeavor even if there's not a consensus about how it plays out in practice. If you've already developed your own definition, and it differs from mine, I hope you'll find something tangible and *do*able in what you read here. I aim to cut through the unnecessary complications and offer an executable way of implementing CX within your company.

PART I: WE'RE DOING CX WRONG

Whether it's the alien in the Introduction or the boy calling out the Emperor's new clothes, we must discuss the logical flaws with some of the things we do in the name of CX. In Part I of this book, I'll draw your attention to some of the operational things we're doing that don't make sense, and then I will propose the underlying reasons why I think we're getting so much wrong...the philosophical root cause. No, it's not just some rail against NPS or some clichéd call to abandon "the way we've always done it." Some of this stuff truly makes no sense, and if we're to make good use of CX as a discipline, we'll have to acknowledge that. If you are already convinced that we can do better, you could probably just skip to Part II. That's where I'll propose not only a new philosophy for the *purpose* of CX but also a tangible and operational way we can make it happen right, through a framework that businesses can use to build an Office of the Customer headed by a Chief Customer Officer.

CHAPTER 1: DOING CX WRONG OPERATIONALLY

Customer Experience is a profession that embraces the concept of taking off institutional blinders and seeing things from a different perspective: that of the Customer. As CX professionals, we're to call out organizational blind spots on behalf of our Customers and see things the way they do; to represent them at the table. It's funny then, the many ways in which we are getting our own profession wrong by not thinking creatively and curiously enough. Here I'll point out a few ways that show that some of what we do as CX champions misses the mark completely.

Vexing VoC

I have a friend (not an alien, but he *does* have an MBA) who *loves* NPS surveys. It's not because he yearns to be asked how likely he is to recommend products and services to his acquaintances but rather because he knows I'm in the CX business. He likes to needle me when he gets the likelihood to recommend question under preposterous conditions. What's more, he relishes giving a response of "*zero*" to these questions in circumstances where he recognizes how silly it is to ask them. He takes the question literally: "How likely am *I* to recommend? Not very...I can't imagine a time or situation when I'd be in a position to do so."

One time he visited a very popular big-box store (you'd know the brand) not far from his house. He truthfully ranked the likelihood as "0" and lined out in the verbatims (the open-text box asking him to explain why he responded with the numerical score he gave) that the experience was perfectly pleasant and he had no problems whatsoever and would likely return *himself*, but that he couldn't imagine any conceivable context in which the question would even come up, let alone him recommending to friends, relatives, or colleagues that they go to this particular store to buy wild bird seed. "What?" he asked, "Do they see themselves as a possible destination for such purchases? Is that what they're going for here with this question?"

To put it bluntly, some of the questions on our surveys are, well ... dumb. What's worse, the more people who answer surveys honestly (although my friend is clearly indulging his snarky side, guileless shoppers no doubt also read the questions as worded and are likely to conclude, and respond, likewise), the more we're likely to whip ourselves into a frenzy wondering why we're turning off our Customers (when in reality we're not). Worse than that, such survey answers prompt us to hold people to account for failures that aren't *actually* failures. How many front-line workers at this store, after all, were sent scrambling over my friend's "0" score? They want to get to the bottom, perhaps, of "what went wrong" with my friend's visit when, in reality, they were just asking him a dumb question.

Overthinking is going on here, and whether you're using NPS, C-SAT, Customer Effort Score, or any other system of top-level CX KPI measurement, likely you're doing so because that's the standard within

4

your industry and among your competitors. Few ever think too much about whether it makes sense or if the questions they're asking will get them the information they need to do a better job on behalf of their Customers. That's the real shame: We put so much mental energy into trying to overthink and crack into our Customers' thoughts to get their inputs on surveys that we overlook the glaring shortcomings of the questions we're asking in the first place. I've worked with organizations trying to drive a higher response rate, desperately wanting to know what their Customers think, thirsty for their feedback, and yet when they get the Customers' attention, they squander it by asking weird questions. Frankly, I'd suggest that in many circumstances, a low response rate is *a reaction to* asking silly questions. Who's got time for *that*?

Our Voice of the Customer (VoC) failings are even more fundamental than that: On the one hand, we over-*think* surveys, but on the other, we consider them the end-all, be-all of VoC, and so we under-*use* them. We rely on surveys as if they are the only way to learn how our Customers feel about us and to understand their experiences. Many organizations aren't actually curious about what their Customers think, and that's why they flippantly toss out a survey every time they interact with a Customer and call it a day.

Don't get me wrong; surveys are an awesome way to put some quantitative meat on the bones of what really is a collection of qualitative impressions: You can count up how many people think this or that, and that can give you a good impression of your overall impact and a broader picture of how Customers feel generally. But those numbers on a chart in a slide are a far cry from showing the *whole* story about how you're impacting our Customers' lives and how they feel about your brand. A whole universe of information lies out there, and all too often, too many brands rely simply on surveys that they're collecting themselves (with boilerplate, incurious questions, let's not forget) to make broad-brush and sometimes rash decisions about what to do with their scarce resources. There's no curiosity, no creativity, in how they gather insights into what their Customers think about their brands and the gaps their Customers see in the delivery of their Brand Promise. They don't realize there's much more to VoC than surveys.

But at least those organizations see the *value* of the VoC, even if they're going about it in a half-hearted manner.

VoC for VoC's Own Sake

An organization can do worse things than collect this limited picture of the Voice of the Customer. There's no sadder thing to witness as a CX professional than a company wasting their resources on a VoC program that's never put to use.

A while back at a conference, I had an illuminating conversation with a COO who was quite proud of her *"CX Program."* She expressed surprise that so few of her peers in attendance were emphasizing ways beyond surveying to gain insights into their Customers' thoughts. She went on at some length about how she had a diverse and dynamic system for listening and reporting on her VoC results. I even took notes on some of the clever ways she went about asking probing questions in her surveys and for that matter using other methods altogether to gain insights beyond surveys themselves. Indeed, I was impressed and congratulated her on these efforts. I asked her what I considered to be the next logical question: "So, then what?" She got even more animated and braggadocious about things.

"Well," she said. "We've instituted a new dashboard that's available to the whole organization and posted it in real time on monitors in the common work areas showing our NPS and supporting background survey numbers as well. We've sped up the reporting cadence and are now briefing the entire leadership team in our weekly meetings. Our company-wide internal newsletter now features a section on CX where we post all the relevant scores and insights including valuable thoughts that come from many different sources of Customer information as well as highlight verbatims from our Promoters and call out outstanding performances by team members." She was nearly out of breath when she finished, so excited by all the progress.

Now, in fairness, she really *was* miles ahead of many organizations I've worked with in terms of sharing and disseminating VoC information, not to mention thinking *beyond* surveys. But I still wasn't hearing what I'd hoped for. So, I pressed again. "That's great," I said. "But besides reporting and sharing, what are you, ahem, *doing* with the results?"

See, this business leader was making the same mistake many folks do when it comes to CX: They're collecting tons of information about the experiences of their Customers, but other than *reporting* the information, they're not doing anything with it. In reality, she was describing simply a *VoC* program, which is only one part—albeit, an important part, and one she was doing a bang-up job of performing—of an overall CX program. She was really missing the whole *purpose* of the VoC though: showing you where you're falling short and where you can improve what you're doing *in order to improve* your Customers' experiences.

It's really a shame too because clearly this COO, her colleagues on the leadership team, and the entire organization were all gaining enthusiasm for Customer-centricity. I imagine all this emphasis on the VoC was having a positive impact on the culture of the organization. That's to be celebrated, even if it's only a partial victory. We briefly discussed how the team's attitude had improved along these lines and then I inquired as to what she intended to do with *that*, this newly discovered interest in "CX" (I called it that, even though it wasn't really CX, but simply VoC). She wasn't quite sure, but she was starting to understand that the energy and attention she was creating around the Customer could actually be put to use toward productive ends, rather than just sitting on a chart even if that chart had the enthusiastic attention of everybody who saw it.

I hear similar situations from my CX colleagues who are trying to make a difference in their organizations. They're hired as experts in Customer Experience, or perhaps promoted into CX leadership roles from Customer support or service departments. Sometimes they take over the "Survey Team" or are working directly with an outside vendor who is helping them develop their VoC programs. But all the efforts end once those numbers come in (and find their way into slides at leadership team meetings somewhere). In essence, they're just glorified (or maybe *not* so glorified) analysis and reporting shops, sometimes not even with that much *analysis* included.

A *lot* goes into developing a robust and insightful VoC program, don't get me wrong. Properly executed, it takes a lot of resources and can cost quite a bit of money to get a good, really meaningful, view of your Customers' impressions of your brand and their experiences with it. That investment, though, is just my point: To take the fruits of that labor and investment of time, resources, and money and simply put it on a slide monthly for a business review is really a waste. Analysts cost *a lot* to hire and retain. Why call it a day once they've done their job, which really should be to feed into something bigger anyway?

As I like to say, if all you're doing is reporting your Voice of the Customer data and scores, CX becomes a lot like the weather: Sure, it impacts you; and yes, everybody *talks* about it. But nobody ever *does* anything about it.

CX Culture Handwaving

We've heard it before: "Our Customers are #1!" Some organizations say they'll do *anything* for their Customers. Some say they're at "The Top," and others have them "At the Center" of all they do. (Well, which is it? The Top? The Center? Out Front?) For an employee of one of these so-called "Customer-centric" organizations, it's sometimes hard to understand what all this means. What's more, sometimes it's hard to square the rhetoric with what they encounter as team members on a daily basis. Remember, their job is to deliver your Brand Promise to your Customers. What does that even mean through all this We-Love-the-Customer word salad?

CX programs can sometimes devolve into so much pabulum and word-mashing. Driving a culture that's truly Customer-centric takes more than just putting up banners and sliding the word "Customer" into a few foundational documents where it seems to fit. For that matter, it's dissonant to deluge your employees with emphatic, but overly general, instructions to prioritize Customers and their happiness but then not provide the tools or engender the atmosphere necessary to take care of the Customers in daily practice.

One common shortcoming of many CX initiatives? Leadership thinks that putting up banners and redrawing the organizational chart as an inverted pyramid with the Customers on top and the CEO at the bottom is all that's required to promote *cultural* change and dedication to Customers. In fact, if not followed up by tangible and observable action, these gestures and words often lead to even *worse* outcomes. Why? Because employees see through the gauzy use of rhetoric not backed up by sufficient resources and empowering policies, and

8

develop cynicism and disengage altogether. As a Customer-centric leader, you can't insist all your employees give 100% of their attention to the Customers if you're not willing to make an investment yourself.

Placards and promotional collateral materials surely are *part* of Customer-centric culture efforts, but if they constitute all the efforts *of* your CX culture program, people will see through it right away and you'll make no progress. In fact, you'll regress.

Also, sometimes leadership will embark on internal Customer awareness campaigns without much *specificity* about what they mean or the goals to be achieved. This can make implementing such work somewhat hollow and meaningless: Be sympathetic and listen to the Customers? Be present, in-the-moment, and search for a positive resolution to their problems? Seek common ground and look for win-win solutions? Gee, thanks, Boss! I learned all that from my kindergarten teacher. Give me something I can *work* with here. If "being Customer-centric" boils down to generalized interpersonal communications improvements and practices, it may improve some transactional interactions. But if it's not tied to a broader brand-based strategy, you're missing an opportunity for differentiation, and team members will be lost looking for guidance more specific than simply "Be polite."

Bluntly put, for example, no call center in the world doesn't have *some* sort of signage imploring all who see it to keep the Customers in mind. But far too few of them explain anything about what that's supposed to signify as relates to the company's overall strategic objectives and Brand Promise. What, after all, does "take care of the Customer" even *mean*?

Likewise, taking care of the *employees* is vital to successful CX efforts. But this can get way out of control too. I've seen a lot of CX programs run aground because companies treat their employees *as* Customers themselves. This is a *huge* mistake, because the sometimes-competing priorities and needs of employees and Customers can lead to a conflict of interest if shared goals aren't established first. Yes, your employees are your most valuable resource and downright essential to the success of your CX program. It's not to take anything away from that to point out that your employees are *not*, in fact, your actual *Customers*. Two things can be true, after all. But the esteem that you hold your employees in should be in service of a greater purpose. Treat your employees like royalty? Sure. But heavy is the head that wears the crown, and their goals should match yours: to serve the Customers. It amazes me how often organizations get this wrong.

It's an important and delicate (but, really, not *that* hard to reach) balance between valuing your employees, and leveraging that value toward the purpose of *serving* your Customers. Organizations blow this all the time, on each side of that scale.

These operational blind spots may be well-known, and even recognized within your organization. Heaven knows, as I speak with business leaders, sometimes simply asking some of these questions ("Why are you doing *that?*" "Why are you asking *that* question?") results in many an *Aha!* moment. But there's something fundamental behind these shortcomings in our execution of CX. A correction can only come when we recognize that we're approaching Customer Experience from the wrong angle—with the wrong understood purpose—in the first place.

CHAPTER 2: DOING CX WRONG PHILOSOPHICALLY

For demonstrative purposes, I'll invent a character named Bob.

Bob was the owner and sole remaining employee (let's use that awesome brick-and-mortar anachronism, "proprietor") of the very last operating Betamax VCR repair shop in the US. I'll offer that, in the last quarter that his business was open, his C-SAT scores (NPS likely hadn't been yet invented) were probably not just good but extraordinary: With fewer Customers, he could give each one special attention and perhaps get to know them personally; he'd been doing this long enough, and having survived the expiration of all his competitors, had plenty of practice to become quite the lone expert; the obvious writing on the wall of the impending collapse of his trade led to a level of sympathy and good will from his remaining Customers; and with nowhere else to go, for that matter, they were pretty much beholden to him for service. Things were, paradoxically, heady and declining at the same time.

I'll go ahead and throw in that perhaps the imminent ending of his profession may have coincided with an approaching of his own retirement age that afforded him a pretty philosophical view of his work and career; this likely translated into a sunny disposition and a good rapport with those who'd visit his little shop. Maybe a national news program even did a human-interest story on him and his business.

Considering all these factors, it's no wonder his Customers gave him positive reviews.

But likely one thing Bob didn't have any trouble understanding, and lost little sleep over the dissonance of: why those fantastic CX scores didn't translate into soaring sales and revenue.

These Metrics Won't Get You There

Bob may not be a statistician, but he didn't outlast his competitors in the Betamax repair business because he was gullible or dumb. He's got a good head on his shoulders for business and knows when to trust his gut. If anybody had come along and promised him a certain percentage increase in sales or revenue directly tied to improvements in his C-SAT score, he'd have been cagey to say the least. And he would have been right to be skeptical.

One of the things that drives me most to distraction as a statistician and a CX professional is the reliance people put in so-called "math" (or worse, "statistics") to improve the bottom line via Customer Experience endeavors. Tons of studies purport to "prove" the relationship between "doing CX" and top-line business KPIs. I've heard promises that revenue or sales or market share will improve *by a defined amount* for every point of NPS a company improves. I guarantee you, if you're selling CX as a straight-line magical key to improving these measures, you're writing checks you have no way of cashing. Similarly, if "CX professionals" are trying to convince you as a business leader that *this* will result in *that*, they're selling you a bill of goods. Let me tell you two reasons why that's not an accurate approach, simply from a statistical point of view.

First, there's what are called *exogenous factors*. In the statistical field of study called Design of Experiment, we're taught to account for (to the best of our ability) outside impacts on tests we conduct. This is an entire branch of statistics that's dedicated to creating an environment wherein only the factors we *intend* to test, in fact, show up in our results. For example, if you're trying to determine what brand of fertilizer yields better results in growing crops, you may divide your garden into a few *zones* and use a different type of fertilizer in each one. But if some of your zones have different irrigation systems or perhaps different exposure to sunlight, these conditions will complicate the results of your experiment and *confound* (Statistics™ term) your results: You'll never be able to determine for sure if the differences in your yield were due to one of these *other* factors, zone by zone. You won't be able to isolate the impact of the fertilizer because other exogenous factors are at play; factors you didn't take into account when designing your experiment. We call it "confounding," and it's bad for statistics

13

and drawing definitive conclusions.

Likewise, in our lines of business, there are things over which we have no control that will impact our ability to market, sell, upsell, re-sell, and sometimes even show up in the market altogether. Just ask Bob about that. We could have a whole discussion about horses and buggies and how entire industries go extinct for reasons that have nothing to do with Customer Experience or Customer-centricity. (Bob likely makes a fortune in retirement speaking on this topic.) And even *within* industries, there are incumbent players who, simply by virtue of their established relationships, greater resources, or mere pre-existence, inhibit or otherwise *prohibit* the performance of newer competitive arrivals. It may be that whatever service or good a company makes is already saturated in the market. It may be that, as a result of a certain widget's commoditization, the market specifically for a *luxury* brand is simply unsustainable anymore. Any savvy business leader will understand this intrinsically and even empirically. But it's nevertheless shocking that so many push against that reality and are *still* looking for that silver bullet regardless of what the market it telling them. Often, CX is determined to be that magic solution. And, oh boy, when it is.

When it comes to exogenous factors, some are *internal*. When you think of brands that are doing well with—and have great reputations for—their CX, another obvious factor emerges. Consider Disney, Ritz-Carlton, Zappos!, and Apple (and I could go on and on): These brands are well-known (and well-studied) in the CX firmament for having exceptional brand loyalty and superb Customer Experience. Notice, also, what they all have in common? They're all *extremely* well-run organizations with strong culture, diverse supply chains, tremendous employee engagement, market-dominating IP, and world-class leadership. Do you suppose any of *these* factors have anything to do with their success? Hmm? Could it be that companies that are generally well-run *also* dedicate themselves extraordinarily to Customer-centricity? In these instances, and many more like them, CX isn't a magic bullet—it's part of an overall arsenal of great business practices. Chicken, meet egg. And it's impossible—and foolhardy—to try to separate them or pick just one as the answer.

The second statistical error people make when they try to predict improved business outcomes like sales and market share based on CX measures and metrics? *Extrapolation.* Here's another example: My friend's son was eight pounds at birth. He and his wife were elated that the boy wasn't over- or under-weight but more or less right at the average for newborn boys. I saw them a few months later and the kid had grown to a stout fifteen pounds. Doing the rough math and wanting to elbow my friend a bit, I said, "Zounds! He's doubled in just a few months. At this rate, he'll be over 120 pounds a year from now!" He had a bit of a laugh, and I said, "Just kidding, of course. He's only growing at seven pounds a quarter. Next year he'll only be about forty." His wife rolled her eyes, unamused, as she knew even *this* estimate was way off. I'm not sure if she knew I was still joking.

Applied to business, and the CX business in particular, again I'm surprised by how many leaders fall for expectations projected based on past experience in anticipation of future conditions that have never been seen.[2] That's not a reason to demure from planning for the future, of course. But it's silly to expect something explicitly based on conditions you've never experienced. If your NPS has never been above 0, for example, how on earth can you suggest what will happen to your business if you start returning +20s or +30s? Aiming for higher, better top-level CX KPI territory is definitely a worthy goal. (And again, here I'm not meaning to specifically call out NPS. My same point contends with C-SAT, CES, or anything else. I'm talking statistics here.) We may even intuit that we'll be doing better, businesswise, when we get there. But if you're being promised, say, a certain return on revenue for every point of NPS you improve, someone's peddling snake oil.

It's safe to say that when your top-line CX KPI improves, you'll likely see some improvement in your top-level sales and revenue numbers. I'm not trying to slay all the dragons at once here: Yes, Customer-centricity *does*, or at least *surely should*, result in better business performance. But there are things like plateaus and (again) external forces that will impede a nonstop reliable and predictable upward trajectory on your financials as your Customer Experience numbers improve. That's not in any way meant to be discouragement from

---

[2] For a controversial but very illuminating perspective on this thought, I recommend anything written by Nassim Taleb. I don't agree with everything he writes, and a bunch of it goes way over my head besides, but he's a great resource for learning about expectations and statistics.

engaging in your CX, nor going full-throttle up. But there will be diminishing returns, somewhere, when you venture outside your historical numbers. Missing that reality is certain to set you up for disappointment in the results, and likely cynicism when it comes to "doing CX" in the future. CX is good. Go for that. But set your expectations reasonably.

Indeed, these sorts of statistical flubs are part of what drove the alien in the Introduction to such distraction. But let's not let our (human) emotions get ahead of logic.

Chasing ROI

I can't blame someone for wanting to better understand the ROI of CX efforts. In fact, dedicating yourself as a business leader to investing in a Customer Experience journey is really kind of sticking it out there. After all, we're all in the business of business to make money, and I don't see anything wrong with wanting to know to what good this is supposed to lead.

But here's the thing: Who's more foolish? The business leader who blows good money after bad on touchy-feely flavor-of-the-month "Hey-let's-all-*do*-CX" business hokum just because it's in fashion or makes him feel good? Or the one who genuinely convinces himself and his entire leadership team (not to mention his Board of Directors and shareholders) that it's going to result in not just sunny uplands of happiness but well-defined tangible, measurable, and reliable monetary results when he knows—if he's thinking properly—that that's not possible, statistically, to promise? Well, maybe that's an unfair question. They're both foolish. At least the first guy can be chalked up as an idealist.

While the former perhaps isn't a very good strategic planner, the latter is going to have a lot harder time realizing his mistake. *He's* the *truer* believer because he thinks he's got the science on his side. What's worse, he's convinced in a way that makes him a hypocrite too.

How so? Watch this:

I'm a big fan of Simon Sinek, of *Start with Why* fame. I don't think he'll come after me for copyright infringement to briefly describe his philosophy: *What* we do isn't as important as *Why* we do it; and the *Why* drives not only the *What* we do but even *How* we do it. There's more to it of course, and regardless of whether you subscribe to his broader ethical and philosophical point, the theory shows up in business all the time. Here's how it applies to our case about CX:

If you want to "do CX" to increase revenue or sales or market share, then your Customers really *aren't* the *most* important thing to you, are they? Not that there's anything wrong with that, but let's be honest. Technically, they're a means to an end: Sure, they're important to you, but they're important to you as a *tool* for greater revenue. You just said so yourself. And in fact, asking the question, "What's the ROI for CX?" is putting it right there as a topic of conversation (and, kind of, exposing your motives). I'm not saying that's not existentially the *truth*. I'm just saying that there's going to be a disconnect if as the boss you turn around and say to your team that your "Customers are #1" to you. They're not, really.

Now, this isn't to be Pollyannaish or otherwise naïve about how business works. I'm not trying to undo business altogether, after all. Without sales, you'll go under. Greater market share is indeed a good thing to strive for. You *do* need revenue to re-invest in your business so you can *even better* serve your Customers. But if you're looking at your NPS and wondering how that's going to impact your sales figures, then NPS isn't really the *top* KPI for you, is it? Turning around and telling your employees that it *is* (and it's what they should be striving to hit) isn't very honest. Believe me, they'll be able to tell.

By the way, yes, I can hear the heads of my fellow CX professionals exploding as they've worked tirelessly to answer that vital ROI conundrum. I'm not here to blow up our spot! And I know that there are *many* organizations (and leaders of those organizations) who won't make *any* move unless they know the payoff in advance. For that matter, I can throw a dart out the window and hit a CX consultant who'll promise such a CX-to-revenue payoff. That's cool, and I know that narrows the appeal for this approach. But it sure does clear away a lot of the confusion about the purpose of CX in the first place to knock down some of these myths.

You may disagree with the philosophy and still want to insist on cash-on-the-barrelhead. But in that same spirit at least, you've plunked down a couple bucks for this book already, so you may as well stick around to see how it comes out. You might even like a few of the ideas ahead.

We may fairly sympathize with Bob the Betamax repair shop owner (a proud guy, he'd likely reject anyone's pity). But one thing that the looming nature of the end of his business afforded him was clarity of thought: He never labored over quantifying the ROI of his CX efforts. He had a pretty specific and even personal relationship with his Customers, and both he and they understood their respective roles in that association.

It also helps that his was always a pretty small shop, without a Board of Directors or stockholders to whom he had to periodically report and present performance metrics and defend his outlays. Surely he had a very fundamental and straightforward understanding and definition of Customer Experience, although he'd unlikely ever have called it by that name.

Bob knew the value of providing a niche service to a specific market segment, working hard to fulfill his Brand Promise, and never taking his Customers for granted. That served him well as far as that business took him, and he was able to provide for his family and then retire comfortably and at peace. Go, Bob!

We're not necessarily that lucky because we're still in the arena. We need a way to make CX make sense.

Likewise, our old friend the alien MBA is still wondering where we go from here. Why, after all, are you still asking that question? What's this "CX" thing all about? What's the point of this, after all?

In Part II, I'll explore a different approach, starting with a more appropriate purpose and definition for CX, then I'll outline a framework for execution applicable to modern, Earth-based companies.

But first, here's a quick guide to tell if you're in need of help:

Part I Checklist: Are you Doing CX Wrong?

☐   Is surveying the only thing you're doing for VoC?

☐   Do the questions, when you survey, not make any sense? Are they boilerplate, completely disjointed from the information you're trying to gather? Do they have nothing to do with your corporate strategy and Brand Promise? Do they provide only a picture of *where you are*, but nothing about *how to improve*?

☐   Are you not doing anything with the insights *from* your VoC program? Are you just reporting the results?

☐   Do you lack a dedicated roadmap of improvement opportunities *based* on your VoC insights?

☐   Is the extent of your "CX Culture" program T-shirts, banners, and swag?

☐   Do you not ask your employees what would help them do their jobs better?

☐   Is your CX team not empowered to take action (and responsibility for those actions) on what they learn are gaps between your Brand Promise and your Customers' experiences?

☐   Are you "doing CX" because you've been sold on its ROI, rather than making it an integral part of your broader corporate strategy?

☐   Do you (or does your team) not even know *why* you're doing CX in the first place?

19

PART II: GETTING CX RIGHT

Between my active service and as a Reservist, I've been in the military now for nearly thirty years. In the military we say not to come with problems, but rather to come with solutions. The spirit is to challenge things that are wrong but also to propose better ways to get the job done. If all you do is the former, you're griping. We need ideas too.

Part I showed ways we are both *doing* CX wrong, and also proposed *why* we're doing it wrong. Rather than just complaining, however, in this part of the book I'll suggest a better way by taking those topics in the opposite order: To frame a solution properly, I'll first propose a more enduring and positive *purpose* for CX along with a definition based on that. Then I'll sketch out an executable framework that we can use to implement CX in our own organizations operationally—a way to *do* CX. You could call it part manifesto, part cookbook.

That ought to get the alien off our cases and on his way.

CHAPTER 3: CX AND STRATEGIC ALIGNMENT: BRAND PROMISE

Whenever business leaders ask me that age-old question about the ROI of CX (or when it comes up in the heady circles of self-described "CX Thought Leadership" I sometimes find myself on the periphery of), I say that line of inquiry misses the point of CX altogether. Then I propose an alternative question:

I'll ask, "Do you think that if your Customers' experiences (see what I did there?) were perfectly aligned with your Brand Promise, *that* would be good for business outcomes? If every time your Customers interacted with your brand, *that* interaction was an accurate reflection and promotion of what you endeavor to be in their lives, that accomplishing this would drive sales and revenue? Do you think that, if you *truly* lived your corporate values and principles, your mission and vision statements—and your Customers agreed, based on their experiences *with* your brand that you were doing so—that you'd improve your market share?" I usually get nods all around the oak table.

Some folks roll their eyes at mission and vision statements or other forms of professions of corporate values. Not me. I'm a true believer in the power of words put into action. In my opinion, there's no use in coming up with these sorts of statements if you're not going to endeavor to live by them. No CEO, no member of a leadership team or Board of Directors worth working with or for is not going to take these things seriously. Likewise, I doubt few would ever answer my line of questioning in the negative: After all, they put those thoughts down on paper and etch them into granite in the lobby of the corporate headquarters because they feel that's the right way to run a business and that's the right way to *succeed* in business. Cynics can laugh at us, but I think we're the larger portion of businesspeople. We agree that alignment is key to success.

So it comes down to this: Are you inclined to acknowledge that having better alignment between your Brand Promise and your Customers' experiences will yield better business results?

Yes, you say?

Congratulations, I tell them, you just sold *yourself* on CX. But let me elaborate.

CX Purpose

Let's start the discussion about CX and the better way to "do" it by developing a better *reason* for doing it, and with that, a better *definition* of it too. Rather than the traditional "ROI" approach, let's start from the more foundational perspective that businesses are all about relationships with your Customers and a greater purpose.

To that end, we develop mission and vision statements, derive a list of principles and values, and define ourselves corporately based on what we *believe in*. Sure, we still build widgets or provide particular services (maybe both), but those are all in line with the purpose of perfecting the role we endeavor to play in our Customers' lives. Here's the rub: *That* should be the purpose of our Customer Experience work, *not* ROI. When we start from there (rather than, say, a promise of windfall revenue), the whole endeavor makes more sense and the results will be better.

For simplicity's sake, I use the term "Brand Promise" to encapsulate not just the mission and vision, principles and values, and other definitive statements about our corporate ethics, but also simply the place in the market we intend to fill. I don't want to trivialize it or oversimplify (and I know I didn't invent that term), but it's helpful to consider all those concepts in one easy-to-define differentiator. After all, they should align amongst themselves anyway, right? Boiling this down to one sentence and labeling it the "Brand Promise" will put the operational pieces of your CX efforts and the role of the Office of the Customer in better perspective, which we'll see in the coming chapters.

For example, your Brand Promise may be that you strive to save your Customers money on their purchases of the goods or services you provide. You're a *discount* brand, or a *value* brand. That's different, of course, from the competitor that strives to provide a *luxury experience* for their Customers. In some ways, in fact, that other provider isn't even *really* a competitor. Sure, you may both be producing more or less the same product, but the *experience* is unique between the two of you, based on what you've chosen respectively as your Brand Promises. Likewise, the Customer segments you're trying to win are different anyway: These are different people. Surely, you'll want to offer the best quality *for the price* of your discount brand. Conversely, that luxury brand will not unnecessarily fleece *their* Customers. But you both have your sights on a particular experience for your respective Customers.

Now, you've likely spent a *lot* of energy and time developing your Brand Promise. It's certainly something that, as the leader of your organization, you've long believed. Perhaps years ago you saw a need in the market for *just* the approach you've developed. Or you were recruited to lead your company and had an immediate attachment based on a shared set of values. Maybe you joined the organization because of those values and rose through the ranks to lead the company. Perhaps any of those scenarios are a bit over-the-top, but in the end, one way or another, you are certainly dedicated to delivering on what your company promises to your Customers. Bottom line here: You're a true believer, and as the leader, you probably *should* be.

So, *that* should be your reason for "doing CX." Just like everything your organization sets its collective mind to accomplish, the Brand Promise is your corporate *Why*: the root of what drives you in the first place. What's nice is that CX, if executed properly, is exactly what it takes to make that Brand Promise real in your Customers' daily lives. Rather than sales, revenue, market share, or other traditional business goals, the ultimate aim of your Customer Experience endeavors should be *to drive alignment* between your Brand Promise and what your Customers experience when they interact with your brand.

I realize this is a totally different way of looking at CX and will upend a lot of notions about it. That's just the point, though, because the value of CX as a discipline is to empower companies to truly live out their missions and visions, their values and principles, their core ideals: That's how you forge lasting relationships with your Customers. And the quest to make that happen also requires a new definition of CX, different from what we've customarily seen.

A New CX Definition

With the understanding that the purpose of Customer Experience is to drive brand alignment, many still ask, "Well then, what *is* CX?"

There are a lot of definitions for CX out there, and with the same humility with which I present anything in this book, I'll acknowledge that the following definition is simply mine. It *does*, however, lend itself to the purpose I just outlined, and allows for executable and operational functions that you can build into the structure of your company. In other words, it provides utility and you can "do" CX as a result. Here it is:

Customer Experience is an enterprise-wide, integrated operation responsible for developing an organization's systems with the goal of aligning Customer experiences with the Brand Promise at every touchpoint.

Let's break down each part of that sentence:

o   Enterprise-wide

Many people "put" CX into a specific department: Customer Service, Customer Support, Sales, Marketing, Customer Success. As we'll see with the other parts of this definition, however, it should have a far reach throughout your entire company if it's to have the intended impact. A CX division within your Customer Care department, for example, can surely do a *lot* of good for improving your Customers' experiences *with that department*, but if that's where it is (more to the point, if that's the extent to where its *influence* is felt because that's where it is), you're really missing a great opportunity. The whole goal of CX is to improve alignment, remember, between your Brand Promise and what your Customers are experiencing. They experience your brand in many ways well beyond any *one* part of your company. In fact, your *entire* company exists to provide value to your Customers, so your CX efforts themselves should be...enterprise-wide.

o   Integrated

This goes along with *enterprise-wide*. It's not enough for every function within your company to have a "CX shop." Sometimes actually that can be overkill or cause confusion. But they all have to be working in concert and be coordinated from a central organization

27

with oversight for that strategy. Each member of your C-Suite oversees a function (and a staff to support it) that's vital to your company. To draw an analogy, each one of them has a budget dedicated to doing their work. Surely each is responsible for the administration and stewardship of that budget. But that doesn't mean you don't need a Chief Finance Officer. The CFO offers not just guidance and information on status but also keeps tabs on those budgets and provides strategic financial guidance for the whole company. CX, just as vital and just as fundamental, likewise needs the disparate efforts throughout the company coordinated and integrated. Your Chief Customer Officer will oversee CX the same way the CFO oversees the finances.

o Operation

Here's a problem a *lot* of companies that try to "do" CX run into: It devolves into not much more than a fad, or at best a temporary initiative. Without actionable plans and goals, CX simply becomes something folks are all talking about. I've got a lot of CX friends who like to insist that "CX is *everybody's* responsibility." Well, yeah, to a degree. But much like I was just saying about *integration*, if CX is *everybody's* responsibility, it's nobody's responsibility (more on that in a second). The point being, if CX is nothing more than a feel-good placing of banners around the office with exhortations to "Put the Customer First!" then sure, anybody can do that (and thus, nobody). You can probably recruit a few people from around the office or maybe create an ad-hoc matrixed team to arrange activities for CX Day every October or have laminates reading, "Yay! Customers!" for everybody to have next to their IDs on their lanyards. (Or, wait! We could put "Yay! Customers!" *on* the lanyards themselves!) But we need to make sure we're envisioning CX as an active, vibrant, vigorous *operation* that, you know, *does* stuff to align our Brand Promise with our Customers' experiences. Remember that? It's the whole *purpose* of CX: *Do* something to *drive* that Brand Promise alignment. That's operational at its core, and it takes an active *operation* to make it happen.

o Responsible

You can't have an operation without giving it responsibility, and you can't have responsibility for anything if there's no operation involved. But something more important is going on here: CX, if

28

done right, will involve the *enterprise-wide integration* of this *operational* work (see what I'm getting at?). I've seen a *lot* of organizations fail at implementing a good CX strategy because they don't give the person and organization responsible for CX the authority to do anything other than report VoC figures or at best *try to influence* process owners to come along and do things better. It's incredibly hard to break down silos within the organization and get a coordinated effort aligned with a CX goal. One way to make that much easier? Set the expectation with the entire leadership team at the outset that the CX team will be *responsible* for the work of improving CX. No "Mother, may I," no begging for resources or information: CX is *responsible* for the improvements, from start to end. (I'll have more to say about this, as it's vital to CX success, in Chapter 9, "Some Parting Thoughts for the CEO.")

o   Developing

I struggled with the verb in this sentence for a while. My framework for CX (which—spoiler alert—you'll see described in further detail in the next three chapters) is predicated on *acting* upon where your Customers are telling you you've fallen short in the quest to make your Brand Promise real to them. That action mostly takes the shape of *improving* your existing business processes. But there's no reason that improvement is the only way to go here: You may need to completely dismantle your processes and *replace* them with better ones. What's more, if you're a new organization, you may not even *have* all of your business processes established or in place. In that case, you'll be *creating* them (maybe even on the fly). That's why, instead, I've chosen the word *developing*. Wherever you are in the maturity of your business, how you do what you do can use improvement, even if you're not even *doing* it yet. So *developing* is what you're doing whether building from the ground up, tweaking what's not exactly perfect, or razing and starting again from scratch.

o   Systems

Likewise, I wasn't sure I wanted to narrow the focus to simply *processes*. It's processes, sure. But it's also tools, practices, policies, regulations, you name it. If it's getting in the way of delivering on your Brand Promise, put it in the dock or on the block. If you're looking at one simple step in a long, arduous chain of requirements, you may be able to break the code and dramatically improve things with just a slight adjustment. I've seen it happen that way. But if, on the other hand, you're taking too restricted a view of how you can improve your Customers' experiences, you may be missing a breakthrough opportunity that could launch you ahead of your industry peers. Improve your processes, sure. But also look at *entire systems*.

o   Alignment (that last bit is all about the purpose)

This shouldn't surprise you. As I stated at the start of this chapter, the whole *purpose* of CX is to drive the alignment between your Customers' experiences and your Brand Promise. Putting this in the definition helps keep that front of mind. Enterprise-wide and integrated, this operation will take responsibility for developing your business systems. Why? To drive your *Brand Alignment*.

So now I've done it. I've upset the applecart. We're now in a new business world where the entire purpose of CX is *not* (simply) to increase sales, revenue, and market share.

I appreciate your hanging in with me this far, and I wouldn't have taken offense if you'd chosen by now to bail. Just like Bob, the Betamax repair shop owner, I know my services and approach aren't for *everybody*. We all have to find our niche. That's the beauty of it: Some brands are discount, some brands are luxury. Some folks want to dip their toes in the CX water and "do" it with a little less structure or definition; some want it to be an active change-making differentiator. It's up to you.

For the fellow travelers along the *purposeful* CX path, we need a map—a picture of where we're going. Basically, we need a *How* to match our newly found *Why*.

The next three chapters will outline these operations: Built upon the foundation of Brand Alignment as the purpose, we'll explore Insights, Process Engineering, and CX Culture. I even drew a picture:

CHAPTER 4: INSIGHTS

One of my favorite shows of all time is *Seinfeld*. In every episode, the characters find themselves in the most preposterous situations one could imagine. (A show about *nothing*? I beg to differ.) I remember one specific episode every time I think of the Voice of the Customer:

Kramer changes his phone number, and the new one ends up being only one digit away from the automated showtimes service, Movie Phone. As a result, he starts receiving lots of misdials. The first couple such calls aggravate him, but Kramer being Kramer ("I've got time" is his rationale), he starts taking calls and answering peoples' questions about movies. As the episode progresses, he really gets into it and puts on an affected voice and invites his callers to, "using your touch-tone keypad, please enter the first three letters of the movie title." Naturally, he has no way of deciphering the series of beeps his callers enter, so after a few incorrect attempts at guessing, he finally says, "Why don't you just *tell me* the name of the movie you've selected?"

That's a *very long* way to demonstrate a point (but I never pass up an opportunity to quote *Seinfeld*): Why do we make it so complicated to ask our Customers their thoughts? If we ask about likelihood to recommend *not* because we're curious about *that* but because we think it's some sort of indication of our Customers' enthusiasm about our brand (and predicted benefits of that enthusiasm), why not just ask *that*? Why not ask them to *tell* us what they think of our Brand?

That alien is onto something: surely there's a better way to do VoC.

Surveys

Just as confused as the alien in the Introduction, Kramer doesn't figure out to simply *ask* the questions he intended until he hits a wall with his callers. We do this all the time with CX. Given that, we shouldn't be surprised that figuring out what to *do* with the quote-unquote *"information"* we get out of our VoC programs is so challenging. Ask a stupid question, as they say.

The solution, frankly, is to stop trying to be so damned clever. One time a CX guru explained to me that the *real genius* about the likelihood to recommend question in the NPS formulation is this: Those who are *really* excited about your brand (i.e., the *Promoters*, those who'd rate you a 9 or 10 on whether they'd recommend your brand to their acquaintances) are more likely *themselves* to come back and spend more. What? I asked if *that* was the whole point: to determine if the *current* Customers, whom you're surveying, would return. He said, "Yeah, that's what's so cool about it!" The real special sauce of NPS? It's a great way to gauge the temperature of your *existing* Customers, and it's those repeat purchases you want, keeping Customers being so much more efficient and all that. So, channeling Kramer, I said, "Why don't you just ask them *that*, then? Wouldn't it be more straightforward and simpler to inquire on your survey if that *particular* Customer—the one to whom you've sent the survey—is going to come back?" I got pretty much a blank look in return.

Frankly, I didn't think there was anything necessarily wrong with the days when everybody was asking their Customers about their *satisfaction*. C-SAT has taken quite a beating over the years. Sure, I can appreciate how some CX champions want more than simply *satisfied* Customers. They want enthused advocates who provide free advertising by telling everybody how great they are. Okay, so tweak it and ask about *how* satisfied they are and strive to drive *that* metric north. ("Are you super-duper satisfied?") More than anything else, enthusiasm and zealotry for the practice of CX led true believers to search for something more effusive than *satisfaction*. A story for another time.

Fundamentally, though, I feel that the origin of all this complexity is an overthinking of why we're asking questions in the first place. As

I stated earlier in the book, by trying to prove the worth and value of CX, we've painted ourselves into a corner—this twisting of ourselves into pretzels to demonstrate the ROI is really why we are trying to *perfectly* formulate *just the right* question for our surveys. If we're trying to convince decision-makers there's an ROI to CX, it's got to be an intricate and complicated design, overlaid with lots of assumptions and connective tissue between formulas. You've got to, as we say in the military, baffle them with bullshit. But if, as I suggest, we adjust the perspective we take on *why* CX matters (that being, to align our Customers' experiences with our Brand Promise), it becomes even clearer that these traditional questions aren't delivering what we need.

How about, instead, if we ask our Customers a question more representative of the true goal of CX?

A Better Survey Question – The Brand Alignment Score

In this spirit, I propose to frame your top-line survey question by first stating—as simply and with as few words as possible—your Brand Promise. Then, ask your Customer how well you delivered on that promise with their last interaction with your brand (or historically, if it's more of a relationship-type survey). We'd call the result the Brand Alignment Score, or since it needs an acronym to seem more official, BAS. You could use a 0-10 scale, a 1-5 scale, even a "You did/You didn't/You *almost* did" scheme. Frankly it doesn't even matter as much *how* you score it (as we'll see in a minute). But for the love of all things decent in this world, *please* stop asking your Customers dumb CX questions that have nothing to do with your CX goals.

Consider this example of how it might work: "At ABC Amalgamated, Inc., our Brand Promise is to deliver the easiest-to-use widget on the market. We strive to make not only our products easy to use but all your interactions with ABC effortless and simple. Based on your most recent experience with ABC, how well would you say we're meeting that promise?"

Notice how straightforward this is. You can interpret *every single* response as either getting the job of alignment done, or not. There's no labored interpretation of probability of whether this person is likely, in fact, to recommend your brand or return for another purchase. It's not a gauge of how much they love or disdain you. It's simply the Customer's opinion (the one that counts, after all) about whether you're living up to what you're trying to be. And yes, if you're the top-level decision-maker, it's still clear that when *more* people acknowledge this alignment you're doing better; that KPI makes good sense.

Most importantly, it's in sync with the whole *purpose* of CX: To drive Brand Alignment.

One important note here to emphasize: *All* survey KPIs are imperfect. By introducing the BAS, I'm not suggesting that it somehow is a much better window *into* the thoughts of your Customers—that same professor who never gave As is also never giving 10s on NPS and is also never going to say, "Oh yeah, 100% to the BAS." That's *not* the problem I'm trying to solve here. If you have the answer to *that* issue (as well as the negativity bias, self-selection conundrums, and any number of other fundamental survey shortcomings), mint it and enjoy your retirement! I'm simply working on fundamentals about how we can correct our *approach* to CX.

Now, a minute ago I mentioned that it doesn't matter how you score (by which I meant, which *scale* you use) the BAS. Why? Because the score doesn't matter *nearly* as much as the insights you gain from asking the right question. Before we move on to other methods of gathering Customer Insights, let me make this final point about surveys: You should ask as few quantifiable questions as possible, and the rest should be asking why that score is so. One common ice-breaker question among CXers is, "If you could only ask *one* question on a survey, what would it be?" For a long time (before I came up with the BAS), I'd cheekily reply, "What sucked about your most recent experience with our company?" I've always been a fan of negative feedback in CX, and not just because it's the only way you can grow by making improvements. The only way you can be sure you know *what* your Customers want you to fix is to let them point it out. In that same spirit generally, you should always be hungry for hearing negative reviews of your brand. You can use your BAS as a top-line quantification to measure your progress, but it's what lies *underneath* that's going to be more valuable anyway.

Score Data and Amplification Data

More specifically, however, it's not enough to have a CX KPI that's in the tank. In fact, you *don't* want that. My point: You're not looking to receive negative *top-line* responses for masochistic reasons, but rather for what you can learn from them. That only happens if they're accompanied by *insights*. That's where the difference between what I call *Score Data* and *Amplification Data* comes into play.

Score Data is, as the name implies, simply that top-line score. It could be a percentage, a weighted percentage, an average, or any way you'd like to calculate it. Basically, it's the number that tells you *where* you are. It's what goes on your dashboard; it's what you compare to how you did last week, last month, or last quarter. There's likely a goal associated with it, and therefore it's the type of data that leadership is usually most interested in seeing. Unfortunately, though, it's also the least useful information you ever get.

The real value comes from what I call the Amplification Data, and that's what tells you *how* you got to the score you received. The Amplification Data is more valuable and insightful, but it is also trickier to collect. You have ultimate liberty to ask for it in any way you'd like. Whether you're using the new, awesome Brand Alignment Score or one of those archaic, out-of-date ones like C-SAT or NPS (who uses *those* anymore, really?), how you come about the data there is pretty straightforward. But in collecting Amplification Data, you have a lot of options.

You can simply follow up your Score Data question with something like, "Why did you score us that way?" That's an awesome way to allow your Customers to have their say in their own words and on their own terms. I recommend leaving an open text box (without a character limit) right below the top-level KPI question and let your Customers have at it. I've taken surveys that allow attachments as well, which is also a great way to uncover hidden gems in VoC data. I've even used that attachment opportunity to upload a .txt or .doc file with my *actual* thoughts because the text box they offer had a limit of too few characters. But Customers can offer pictures or video of what happened to their products, samples of work, or other things in lots of different formats that will not only allow you to address *their* issue (if it's still open), but see what it looks like from their perspective so you can better address what's going wrong *systematically*.

There's a place where Score Data and Amplification Data collide, however. As I just mentioned, I'm particular to open-text (and unstructured data of other formats as well) because it's less restrictive and therefore more robust and rich with insights when it comes to collecting Amplification Data. The insights collected in these formats are a bit more complicated to quantify (although new artificial intelligence and machine learning products and services are coming online all the time to help you with this analysis), but doing so can help point you in the right direction to determine which systems within your organization are failing and how. Often, when patterns emerge, organizations will alter their survey questions to take account for that. Usually, it's because having identified an issue, they want to track it and monitor the frequency of certain *types* of failures. That's natural and probably a good thing. It'll usually take the form of a follow-on question used to identify the *type* of issue or failure: Was it the product's materials? Was it the product's durability? Was it the product's look and feel? Was it the delivery? These more specific Amplification Data questions (normally in a drop-down style format) are likely the result of investigations that found a few main causes for bad CX that a brand wants to track.

This can be a very efficient way to account for problems and track the progress of improvements. I wouldn't necessarily recommend *against* this, but be aware of and on the lookout for a few caveats and warnings with doing so.

First, keep in mind that you're narrowing the Customer's options to share with you what went wrong. Depending on how restrictive your response options are, your Customer may not have any way of offering you meaningful feedback. If you're going to use this approach, always offer an option for "Other" with a free-text invitation to elaborate.

Secondly, and related but in the more positive direction, I've seen people offer surveys to Customers (or potential Customers) asking for their thoughts on offerings or features along the lines of "Which of these would you be interested in seeing from us?" After that, there's a collection of things *the brand* had already thought to offer. This approach is bad because not only does it restrict the Customer's options, it turns into what we in the statistics world call a *self-licking lollypop*: "Guess what, folks! The Customers *love* our proposed ideas! 80% of them said they want us to offer this upgrade!" Of course they did, but did you ask them to prioritize your offerings? What might they want *more* but weren't offered as an option?

Another reason it's risky to take this course? You can lose sight of emerging issues. If you're asking your Customers to categorize their issues based on what you heard last year but haven't done a reassessment of what's going on *now*, you're likely missing new problems. Also, you're probably unnecessarily patting yourself on the back for having so successfully taken care of your main drivers of dissatisfaction. You may wonder why your Score Data doesn't reflect your Customers' happiness with your hard work, but that's because there's now something *else* that's impacting it more than what you've fixed. It's a *good* thing that you've fixed that previous issue, but now it's got to be on to the next!

Finally, as with anything in business, what gets measured gets managed. That's a corollary to a law I invoke all the time with clients, Goodhart's Law: "When a metric becomes a goal, it ceases to be a good measure." The point of this adage? We can get carried away in how we interrelate our Score Data and Amplification Data. If we convince ourselves (sometimes accurately, sometimes inaccurately) that a certain *score* is driven by a particular underlying failure, we're likely to make improving *that problem* (or at least the manifestation of the problem in its measure) a priority. That's a great approach, and I often recommend it. However, fast-forward a few months, and some people become so intent on attacking the specific problem (or more accurately, the *measurement* of how that problem is coming along) that they lose track and perspective of why they're doing it. They'll do anything they can think of to drive that number (the one that measures what's been determined as the root issue) in the right direction even if doing so actually drives the *score* metric in the *wrong* direction. Call it the tyranny of focus.

I knew of a contact center whose agents were quickly (oftentimes poorly) diagnosing a Customer issue, giving instructions on what to do, and telling the Customer to call back if that didn't fix the problem. Repeat calls were through the roof, which was leading, in part, to poor CX. But average handle time (AHT) was stellar! It didn't take much digging to find out how *that* happened: I discovered that the offending contact center had previously determined that AHT was the driving factor in poor CX. Fix *that*, they figured, and CX will follow. Clearly that was *not* the case. Concentrating on AHT (instead of the actual *experience*) led to a myopic approach that ended up *harming* the Customer experience instead of helping.

Another extreme example of Goodhart's Law: when people take unethical means to drive that "root cause" metric toward the goal or fudge or otherwise manipulate the data or its collection to make it *look* better. Obvious circumstances of that go without saying, but you'd be surprised how many times I've seen people with the best of intentions, for example, adjust the manner in which they collect data or perhaps re-categorize Customers into different types so they can exclude some negative results from the top-line numbers. Goodhart has odd and unintended consequences. This isn't a reason *not* to try to focus your search, just something to be aware of.

Beyond Surveys

But let's talk about things *besides* surveys because one of the biggest (but certainly not *the* biggest, as we'll see in the next chapter) mistakes people make with their insights programs is relying solely on surveys. No doubt surveys are an excellent and efficient way to determine what your Customers think. As I just discussed, there are a *lot* of drawbacks, but many of them can be addressed by way of being smart about how you survey. But there are still lots of insights out there that you simply can't get from surveys no matter *how* cleverly designed and conducted.

Keep in mind the importance of looking for creative ways of finding gaps between your Brand Promise and what your Customers experience with your brand. Those insights won't necessarily come in the form of easily quantified survey results, so you have to go out and get them from other sources as well.

For example, you can supplement or improve upon the limited insights you're gaining from your surveys by simply picking up the phone and calling your Customers. While surveys are great because they're anonymous, their results often lack the depth you can get when you're speaking directly with your Customers and can follow up on what they say. In that moment, it surely makes more of a difference in that they realize you're taking their feedback seriously (it's more personal than an automated survey, oftentimes sent by a third party); you're strengthening that bond between your Customers and your brand. But also, the responses are much more robust and offer much more actionable intelligence.

You can't interview nearly as many Customers as you can survey, but it can be a good augmentation based on either following up or simply making a practice of interviewing a few every now and then. Many organizations have a recovery department responsible for wooing back Customers who've cancelled their service. I worked with one company whose recovery function wasn't doing well in retaining Customers. I suggested they start using the process to better understand what they could fix *systematically* in their processes rather than just trying to recapture *this particular* Customer. The insights they gained from this approach offered a ton of improvement opportunities. Addressing these issues meant they didn't recur for *other* Customers, so there wasn't any need to try to retain them—they never got upset to begin with. By all means, pick up the phone and interview your Customers, especially the ones who are disappointed. You may save that one Customer, but the insights you gain from that experience may keep you from losing future ones.

Additionally, there's this thing out there the kids are using called the *Internet*. Maybe you saw that movie with Sandra Bullock. It's been a while since she made it, so let me catch you up if you've not been following events since then. Online forums and review sites are a treasure trove of feedback you can get that has one very important characteristic: It's unfiltered. Even if you're sending out blind surveys, your Customers may not be telling you what they really think (I know, surely some of your responses put the lie to *that*, but it's true). For some reason, people are a *lot* more forthcoming about your shortcomings if offering it up freely instead of you prompting it.

Someone on your Insights team should be monitoring review sites to see how, not only your Customers are reviewing you, but also how those reviews are being received. Even when you're not mentioned, sometimes you can glean a lot from what your Customers want based

41

on feedback they offer about your competitors. At the end of the day, observing your Customers "in the wild" and without prompting can be a great source of insights. Likewise, similar to the aforementioned recovery calls, sometimes you can dual-purpose these forums by wading in yourself if you find active problems you can fix on behalf of particular Customers. Lots of brands already do this, but don't lose sight of the insights you can gain by looking these over.

Speaking of technology, you may not even have to bother your Customers to gain insights into what they think about your goods or services. In the new economy where nearly everything, it seems, is being sold *as a service* (XaaS), many—if not most—interactions with your Customers will occur *right on your own systems*. If you're offering a Software as a Service business model, you literally have your Customers logging into your IT infrastructure all the time. You likely monitor their activity and comings and goings. Obviously, you want to respect their privacy and abide by your own terms and conditions— I'm not talking about snooping. But if you notice that a Customer of yours hasn't logged in to your program in several days but used to do so several times *per* day, there may be a loss in perceived value.

If you're selling access on a subscription basis to some sort of service, a great sign of potential churn would be a Customer no longer using the services that much, wouldn't it? There may be other explanations, but if a Customer's use suddenly drops off, it's likely a good sign of lost interest or diminished perceived value of what you're providing. So, crack that usage data open and look for bends in the knee: See if a certain segment of your Customer base has lost its taste for what you're offering, or if perhaps you're losing them to a competitor who's delivering more, better, faster, or whatever they're looking for. The point is, the data at your fingertips won't necessarily provide you with all the answers for what might otherwise be a swell of lost Customers, but it can give you an idea of where to look (not to mention a heads-up, perhaps, before it happens).

Also consider using focus groups. You may not have access to two adjoining rooms with one-way mirrored glass between them, but some companies do. They charge for the use of their facilities (and I'd recommend using their services too), but it's well worth it to witness your Customers and potential Customers interacting with your product or potential product. Other, less elaborate forms of focus group sessions and analysis can be performed, and you don't always have to hire from outside to make this happen. Just remember the whole purpose is to be curious about seeing what your Customers think about your brand. If you start with the right spirit in mind, you'll likely get lots of good insights.

Less elaborate is the concept of secret shoppers. You can hire people (there are a *ton* of folks in this niche field) to experience life as your Customer and then produce a report about where you're falling short and what you need to improve. What's great about this is that these people are, to coin a phrase, *professional* Customers. They know what to look for, sometimes even better than your real Customers, because they're deliberately trying to identify whether you're living up to your Brand Promise. They can also shop your competitors and let you know how you stack up against them. This can be incredibly valuable for perspective.

Finally, I never let a conversation about Customer Insights pass without mentioning walking in the Customers' shoes. Often, I've professed that if, for some reason, you had to choose only *one* activity from among all the different forms of VoC, I'd recommend this one. There is no better education than experiencing your processes *yourself* from the Customers' perspective. Customers can gripe about what a pain in the neck your website is all day long, and you can convince yourself that they're all just being unreasonable. But there's one way to put the issue to rest for sure: Log on yourself. (Or try to!)

In Brad Stone's book about Amazon, Jeff Bezos, incredulous about assurances from his Customer Service VP that phone wait times were minimal, dialed up the number right there in the middle of a leadership team meeting. That didn't work too well for the claim, but more importantly, it shows how much more meaningful and impactful it is to walk through the processes your Customers are forced to use than it is just to look at charts and graphs in a PowerPoint slide show. Sometimes it can be esoteric (perhaps you only see one *part* of the process, or perhaps you encounter *one team member* who's genuinely having a bad day), so the *precise* results should be taken with a grain of salt. But every person on the leadership team should be required to walk in the Customers' shoes.

Another benefit of experiencing what your Customers face is that, if you're already using the more traditional methods of VoC (surveys,

43

interviews, etc.), you can go out and purposefully look for the experiences your Customers are already telling you about. This deliberate approach can help clarify just what's meant and also drive home those points about ideas and opportunities for improvement.

Some organizations go to *Seinfeldian* lengths to determine the Voice of their Customers, unnecessarily convoluting themselves in order to identify *just* the right piece of information they can use to derive insights.

I admire and appreciate the curiosity that shows. Far too many folks fall into the other extreme: They don't really bother trying to figure out what their Customers think at all. But there's really no mystery, when it comes to surveying: Ask questions based on the purpose of your CX efforts. The Brand Alignment Score will give you a great starting point as a top-level KPI when it comes to seeing how you're improving or sliding in living your values in your Customers' eyes.

But don't stop there either: Dig deeper in what you ask, and be creative in *how* you gain this insight in order to identify not just *where* you are, but *what* you can do about it. We'll investigate that *what* next.

CHAPTER 5: PROCESS ENGINEERING

I have a great friend in the CX world named Nate Brown. He's been in CX for a long time, under some challenging circumstances in fact, and rightly holds a place of esteem among many of us in this profession. One of the things I admire most about Nate is his dogged emphasis on action in the practice of Customer Experience.

Frequently, Nate reminds us all that Customer Insights are *not* the end of your CX work but rather the *beginning*.

As I mentioned earlier, it's a tremendous waste of resources to work tirelessly to better understand the place your brand holds with your Customers and where you're falling short of the mark but never to put that insight into action. If you're only reporting your VoC, you don't have a CX program. Improving what you do in order to *move* those numbers is the only reason you should ever collect that information. Consider these thoughts on *how* to do that.

Do Something!

Operations Research is a field of study with its beginnings in the military. It has a long history of driving efficiency and using hard facts and measures to improve processes and systems. The bold among us who study it call it "The Science of Better." While that fits nicely on a T-shirt (one of which I owned back in grad school), it really is a fascinating endeavor and makes big contributions not just in military uses but also in business and industry. I'm not sure if there's a direct line of progeny, but it's the study of Operations Research and other applied statistical fields (Industrial Engineering, Systems Engineering, and other types of engagement) that lend themselves to what I'll categorize here as Process Engineering (PE).

In the business world, Process Engineering encompasses skills such as Six Sigma, Lean, Kaizen, Design Thinking, Change Management, and other *making-things-better* tools and approaches. Most of these have had heydays, champions, burnouts, and resurgences. Some, like Lean Six Sigma, join forces for good. Yes, like many things in business, they come and go. There are differing levels of adoption, various appeals, diverse degrees of sophistication and rules, and, of course, *tons* of certified professionals, experts, and gurus. I am, for example, not only a Lean Six Sigma Black Belt but also a Certified Scrum Master, a Certified Quality Engineer, and even a recovering PMP from the Project Management Institute. There's enough doctrine out there to choke a horse, and frankly, I couldn't care less which approach you use or what you call it. The real important thing here is to improve your processes and systems.

Invent your own, in fact. At one point in my career, I spent all my days delivering workshops teaching Lean Six Sigma as well as Agile/Scrum and various other techniques, both internally and as an independent consultant. I'd always point out to workshop attendees that at the end of the day, in these disciplines, there's really nothing new under the sun. Each tool I'd introduce to the class, I'd have someone pop up and say, "Oh yeah, we used that tool once for a project I was leading," or, "That's not what we call *that* tool on *my* team." I'm not pulling back any curtains to reveal industry secrets by noting that most of these approaches are simply a collection of tools made easy to remember with an acronym or otherwise logically categorized within a rational series of steps. That's not to denigrate or disavow the value of these frameworks and methods—quite the opposite. Sometimes, simply having the array of tools lined out within an easy-to-understand and -follow framework makes the difference between not even knowing where to start on one hand and having a coherent roadmap to success on the other. So, pick one that makes sense to you, or a creation of your own, as long as your team can use it to improve your processes.

The bottom line is that if your CX efforts are going to succeed, you'll need to *act* on the insights your Insights program delivers.

Organizations typically use PE when the leadership recognizes a need to improve efficiency and quality. Sometimes, waste or errors within your processes cost you much more than they should. Lean, Six Sigma, Kaizen, and all these others, are great tools for rooting out waste in your processes (the Japanese call it "muda," one of many Japanese terms Lean practitioners like to toss around). Some of the approaches are more concentrated on reducing the *variation* in your processes to make them more reliable. The results can be a much more efficient and effective organization. This opens up resources (since, being more efficient, you don't need them for wasteful processes) for valuable endeavors such as R&D, product development, innovation, or simply growth and scaling.

Unfortunately, of course, lots of organizations prefer to pocket the newfound slack in their systems by identifying redundancies and even laying people off. It's kind of a slap in the face when your boss says, "Thanks for helping us lean out the processes here. As a result of your hard work, we've realized we don't need you anymore. Buh-bye." It's sad (and, in my opinion, a very stupid way to do business), but it happens. A *lot*. And it gives Process Engineering, as a discipline, an undeserved negative reputation. Believe me, if this has ever happened to you, trust that they're doing it wrong.

Now, I came to Customer Experience, in fact, by way of my Lean Six Sigma background. I got my first CX job when a former student in one of my Executive Belt classes (which my team developed to instruct leaders on the value of LSS and how to be a successful champion and sponsor for PE efforts within their organizations) approached me and asked if I'd lend that expertise to the goal of improving his Customers' experiences. In my mind, that was revolutionary. Even if an organization isn't so short-sighted to simply lay off people thanks to the newly freed resources from their PE efforts, there's no doubt that the main purpose typically is to save capital. Use it however you'd like, but businesses don't normally put all their work into improving their processes simply because the results *look* more elegant and streamlined. No, they do it to save or make more money. That's something you can get behind, as long as you're not the one facing a layoff as a result.

"But wait," I said. "You want to use these efficiency tools to improve your *Customers'* experiences? Now *that's* a flag to rally around!"

Before I go on here, I have to acknowledge that, yes, Lean, Six Sigma, and all these tools and approaches are *nominally* Customer-centric. For example, in the definition of that Lean term "muda," work that does not *add value* is considered waste. That *value* is defined, explicitly, as "what the Customer is willing to pay for." So, it isn't as though the whole effort is centered around internal desires to squeeze cost out of the processes, Customers notwithstanding. In fact, they are integral to the definition. Even there, though, you can see that the bottom line is still green, as it's not that Customers simply *want* something but rather that they value it enough that they're willing to *pay for* it. Nevertheless, there are still lots of examples of PE initiatives that may never even take the Customer into account; they're simply efforts to save money. There's nothing wrong with that; after all, we're all in the business of business to make money, and you can't survive long if you're not operating efficiently.

That said, though, it's much more of an inspiring sentiment around which to roust a team (and bring your whole company!) to say that we're going to improve our processes and systems *explicitly* to benefit our Customers and bring a better alignment between our Brand Promise and their experiences. People will find *that* much more stirring than simply squeezing out inefficiencies for the sake of saving some bucks. Ask your team members which of those two themes excites them more. (And leave out the possibility that, if money is the goal, it might be that the savings may come from their own salaries and benefits packages!)

What's even better, of course, is that you really needn't choose anyway. It's not like you have to pick potential improvement opportunities that benefit the Customer *or* the bottom line. That's the beauty of it all—even as you're keeping your eye on costs, prioritizing your PE projects based on your VoC scores instead of financials will still deliver on the latter. There will surely be times when, between two competing initiatives (for your time, your resources, your attention), one would save you more than the other but not deliver quite as much of a boost to your CX. You have to choose which one to pursue. What's great here is that, all things equal, by choosing the project that improves your CX, you'll likely also drive retention, repeat Customer activity, attract new Customers, and make more sales. You're saving money on one end (because you're improving your efficiency and therefore the resource use of your processes) and *making* money on the other (because improved CX will drive more business your way). It's win-win.

Naturally, sometimes the potential savings will be so incredible for a particular project, even if it's not as directly applicable to your Customers' experiences, that you can't pass it up; and I'm not going to second-guess such a great opportunity to apply these impactful tools and make a breakthrough improvement. If it's that big of an advance, it'll likely trickle down to benefit your Customers as well. But on the whole, prioritizing your PE efforts based on how they'll move the dial on your top-level CX metrics is going to end up benefiting you the most. It's much more likely to drive engagement and enthusiasm, and it's not as though it won't save you resources once implemented in and of itself.

Plus, by *using* your Customer Insights by way of *doing* things to fix and improve your processes, you won't be wasting any resources in gathering that feedback. Remember, VoC is only as good as the improvements it leads to.

As a dinner party host, you wouldn't ask your guests about food allergies and sensitivities and then ignore what they tell you. While it may not be as acutely risky from a health perspective, it's at least just as disrespectful to ask your Customers what they think if you have no intention of acting on what they have to say.

Too many organizations think that CX is nothing more than surveys. As I outlined in the previous chapter, even *VoC itself* is more than just surveys. But it's vital to take my friend Nate's recommendation seriously that you will be wasting all your efforts collecting the Voice of the Customer if you don't do something with the results. I think he'd agree with Pablo Picasso, who said, "Action is the foundational key to all success."

What's more, taking action goes a *long* way toward building an enduring and powerful Customer-centric culture in your organization. And that's the topic of the next chapter.

CHAPTER 6: CX CULTURE

I may quote Seinfeld and Picasso and tell stories about aliens, but at my core I'm simply a cold, hard-hearted military analyst. I come from a world that's more concentrated on tangible and countable things, so culture has always been a tough one for me. What's more, Customer-centric culture had to be 100% human (sorry, aliens). This wasn't the sort of culture that I have become used to in the military of teamwork and tenacity. Yes, that was *part* of it, but in building out a CX culture, its fundamentals have to be centered on how we interact with and appeal to our Customers. It's about sympathy and seeing things from their perspective. After all, as a CX leader, it's my responsibility to lead an organization that is supposed to *represent* the Customer within our company.

Your CX culture efforts can't simply be about hanging up signs and banners around the office harping on everybody to "Put the Customer First!" or, more gently, "We [heart] Our Customers!" There's a place for that, sure, and internal messaging, marketing, and education are important parts of this work. But I knew there had to be more to it than *Be Polite* classes and T-shirts.

To that end, when I found myself in a leadership position responsible in part for driving the CX culture, I needed some sort of roadmap. I'm talking about something executable that I could use as a clipboard checklist, so to speak. Unsatisfied with what I was seeing out there and having already built some of the framework you're reading here, I decided to create my own. Customer-centric culture, I surmised, had to consist of three particular aspects: Enablement, Empowerment, and Encouragement.

Oh. I guess it needed *alliteration* too.

Enablement

One of the most ubiquitous posts I come across on LinkedIn? The newly hired employee having snapped a picture of the onboarding kit on his or her first day on the job: New computer, badge, phone, usually some swag, like a travel mug, mousepad, maybe a T-shirt, and, for some reason, lots of branded stationery. While I'm happy for the individual's new beginning, I often wonder: What's *on* that computer?

When we talk about *tools* at work, we don't usually mean hammers and screwdrivers. And for the most part, all we really need are those things we're issued on day one. As time goes on, more paraphernalia gets added to our daily routine: The team uses a particular app or program to keep tabs on each other's work; there's a knowledge base program; and likely also workforce management software for scheduling and HR needs. Sometimes, depending on your job, you come across something new that could help you accomplish your work. If you've ever been to a conference, they're almost always sponsored by someone trying to sell things to people in your industry to make you more impactful at work. Talk about swag!

As leaders, we're obligated to enable our teams with all the tools necessary to carry out their jobs. Some might say that this is leadership's *primary* responsibility: Put the necessary things into the hands of the people who do the work and then get out of the way. Of the Ten Principles of Servant Leadership attributed to Robert Greenleaf, one is Stewardship. If you're responsible for a team accomplishing a goal, the principle goes, the proper acquisition and application of resources is a huge part of your job.

With all the complexities of balancing competing personalities, defusing conflict, managing the intersection of dispositions and jobs to get done, it's amazing how many bosses miss this one very straightforward obligation. It's as though the pendulum of business leadership has swung from the extreme of not caring about your employees, treating them all as automatons, cogs in the machine, to engaging so directly in their lives as to forget, oh by the way, that they have a job to accomplish at work too. Some of the most thoughtful, sympathetic, dynamic and inspiring bosses I've had were shockingly bad at simply arming me with what I needed to do my job. For all the effort and heart it takes to show true compassion for your employees, there's one thing you can do to make them and your team more productive, and you don't even need to be a nice person to make it happen. (Still, though, be a nice person!)

Sometimes it's beyond even your capability to provide the needed tools. One time, I held a leadership position *at a computer company* (an important part of the story) and had to jump through hoops to procure the hardware one of my business analysts needed to do his job effectively. It's a cultural thing, and the attitude that whatever you need to accomplish the job of delivering the best version of the Brand Promise to the Customers has to come from the top. Accountability, adhering to regulations, and following the rules are important parts of running a tight ship. These are also good leadership characteristics. But if they impede your team or otherwise keep it from doing its job, the policies should be investigated and possibly revamped.

There's no excuse for initiating a CX program, spinning everybody up into a frenzy of Customer-centricity, talking big about it, then not enabling your teams with the necessary tools, programs, policies, and systems to put the Customer first in practice.

The bottom line here: You have to put into the hands of your team members all the tools necessary to take care of your Customers.

Empowerment

Almost as bad as not enabling your teams (coming in a *very* close second as it still leaves open the possibility of getting *something* accomplished through your team members' own tenacity and grit), is enabling your employees with tools but not sufficiently *Empowering* them to use them. I don't suppose I need to use an *internal* example of this bad business practice as I'm sure the reader has at some point been a Customer on the phone with a frontline agent who lacked the authority to do something that seemed pretty straightforward. Far too often, it seems, every time you need a replacement, a refund, some sort of exception made, it's, "Please hold [again, but this time] for a supervisor." Sometimes, just to save myself the aggravation of having to repeat myself to the higher level of authority (another thing that always seems to be part of the process), I'll ask the person who answers the phone if he or she even *has* the authority to do what I'm hoping to have done. If not, I'll offer a (very) brief description and just ask politely to be transferred to a supervisor right off the bat. Why waste the agent's time (and drive up the AHT!) if I know I'll need an escalation anyway?

Not enabling your front-line employees demonstrates a lack of trust in them, your Customers, or worse, both. When you don't allow your front line to address as much as possible, you're saying that the rules are more important to you than your Customers' experiences. Well, who wrote those rules? Who are they meant to serve, anyway? You're sending a message.

When your rule requires an escalation to, say, issue a refund or honor a promise, it's likely been put in place to protect the company from those who may take advantage of them. Customers trying to get away with something or exploit a generous offer or lax return policy may unethically attempt to sneak something past the agent. A lazy, distracted, or sloppy agent may inadvertently give away too much or make an offer without properly charging the Customer. So, to keep this from happening, you put policies in place that require a more seasoned team member to review the circumstances before taking action.

But how much risk is there, really?

Lots of brands have very generous return policies (L.L. Bean, Land's End, Trader Joe's, and Kohls' come to mind off the top of my head). They don't just survive, but thrive, in part because of the mutual respect, trust, and loyalty that policies like these engender. These brands turn return policy on its head: Rather than defaulting to a "no" response and then requiring the Customer to do a song and dance to demonstrate worthiness to get a refund, they say "yes," and keep tabs in case someone here or there seems to be gaming the system. When your default is "yes," you don't need an escalation. When you don't need an escalation, you're saving your Customers time, hassle, and aggravation. Oh, and you're in turn making them like you more and trust you *back*. That's never a bad thing. Empowerment works on a lot of levels.

This isn't just about Customer Support though. Often, sales are filtered through a supervisory layer before being approved. Some organizations also have their technical support teams siloed based on differing Customer needs and assigning certain cases to particular teams and issues to different experts. In these cases, some agents aren't even allowed to address certain problems they're capable of fixing. Instead they are told, "That's not your job" (a message that gets passed on to the Customers who call). Any policies that prevent your team members from solving issues or addressing Customer concerns at the earliest and most direct possible contact are an unnecessary complication in the journey of your Customer getting something done.

Even if you're not a touch-feely sort of boss, ultimately another awesome thing about empowering your employees is that it's efficient. Saying "yes" instead of running the gauntlet of your return (or discount, or refund, or whatever) process not only saves your Customers time and frustration and your employees friction, but it's all over much sooner. Your agents can get on to other calls, you can move on to other issues, and your supervisors don't have to spend all their time making "exceptions" and circling back on forms and procedures. Say "yes" and move on!

Now, in fairness, this is easy for me to say: I'm a Customer Experience consultant, so, of course, I want you to put everything into it! But I should acknowledge that, just like with putting in place a PE team—as I recommended in the previous chapter—these policies come with a cost. From the beginning, these costs should be built into the long-term expectations for every new product or service you bring online. Get the CFO on the phone!

Look hard at these policies (yes, sometimes you *do* want to force an escalation) and determine whether the culture you're promoting is one of empowerment.

Encouragement

Once, as a member of a leadership team, I had a boss who was fanatical about focus. That isn't meant to be a criticism (although sometimes the members of the team felt a *little* overwhelmed by his, um, *enthusiasm*). One of the most impressive aspects of his leadership style was to purposefully dedicate our attention, efforts, time, energy, and even resources toward priorities for the organization. If something came up that was vital to our success or perhaps an initiative came down from above, or if an issue arose, we'd do a notional assessment of how this should fit into our existing priorities. Then we'd adjust, as seemed appropriate, allocating our energies to the most important needs. At times, he'd even create and fill new leadership positions and staff whole new organizations, either hiring from outside or promoting within, to oversee the success of these important goals. It was a marvel to see this sort of walk-the-talk leadership in action.

When it comes to building out a truly Customer-centric culture, it's easy, on the other hand, to fall into the trap of simply talking the talk. While Enablement and Empowerment are a lot more straightforward and easier to define and execute, the third E, *Encouragement*, is trickier. That's because many can interpret encouraging our teams to simply be attaboy rhetoric and perhaps at most recognition of great work. Sure, coaching is involved too when team members fall short, and a general sense of teamwork and goal-orientation is a good step as well. Frankly, some organizations simply feel that putting up banners that tout how important our Customers are (or *should be*) is enough to encourage a Customer-centric culture. Don't get me wrong, those banners *are* important and *do* have their place. Same for organizing those CX Day events and an overarching theme of Customer-centricity throughout the office. (And don't forget the T-shirts!)

But as with my former boss, there's tremendous power in putting your money where your mouth is. I don't even just mean that metaphorically, since it *does* cost money. Surely hiring a Chief Customer Officer and staffing an Office of the Customer sends a very strong signal that you're serious about CX: It's not cheap, especially if you're doing it right. Moreover, investing seriously in your Insights program can demonstrate that you're willing to prioritize learning where you're falling short with your Customers and taking steps to improve. And hiring Black Belts and Green Belts can be costly too. Naturally, of course, those *We-love-our-Customers* banners aren't free either.

That said, as a leader, you also send a strong signal when you spend your time and energy trying to understand how well you're living out your Brand Promise in your Customers' eyes, and how improvement initiatives that are in place to better drive that alignment are going. People notice what the boss notices, and when they see the leadership team getting behind PE projects *explicitly* chosen to drive Brand Promise alignment, they can tell it's a priority. As Ralph Waldo Emerson famously (is said to have) said, "What you do speaks so loudly, I can't hear what you're saying." My old boss could have passionately talked and talked about how important this or that new issue may be to the very survival of our organization and company and left it at that. But him focusing on it, making decisions based on it, and driving the entire organization and our resources toward it made an indelible impression: We should *all* prioritize this.

Just so, it can work with CX in your company: Illustrate your commitment to Brand Promise alignment with your Customers by communicating the *work* being done to improve your Brand Alignment Score. Have a dashboard of initiatives that have been specifically selected (and put in priority order) based on what will most positively impact this alignment. Celebrate those successes, and through your actions make clear that this is a continual process.

Another important part of Encouragement: Listen to your team members who have the most contact with your Customers about how you can better arm them to accomplish their jobs. Enablement and Empowerment ideas will most often come from (possibly frustrated) front-line employees who are sometimes begging for help to make your Customers' lives easier. Just as you listen to your Customers and act on what you hear via your Insights and PE programs, do the same with your employees. After all, they've got some of the best insights into how your Customers are dealing with gaps between your Brand Promise and their experiences because they're most likely to hear about it, unfiltered and directly from them on a regular basis.

Even emotionless aliens (at least the ones who go through business school and get an MBA) appreciate these sorts of leadership traits. It's easy to talk a good game about how important the Customers are to you. But as I emphasized earlier, banners up in the workplace and T-shirts handed out extolling how important our Customers are to us are no substitute for taking *action* based on an overarching CX goal of aligning your Brand Promise with your Customers' experiences.

I surely don't intend for this to be the last word on Customer-centric culture or what it takes to build one inside your organization. I'm not an organizational psychologist or a group-dynamic expert.

But I've found that, by keeping these three goals in mind—Enablement, Empowerment, and Encouragement—we can concentrate and emphasize the work we do toward keeping our Customers at the center of our work environment in a way that keeps us focused on making our Brand Promise real our Customers' daily lives.

If you've embraced the connection between your Insights and PE programs (insights leading to action), try mirroring that approach internally with your employees' feedback and that will be a good first step. In much the same way, your CX culture program should include listening to your employees ("What do you need to better do the job of delivering our Brand Promise for our Customers?") and acting on what you learn (putting in place the necessary systems, tools, and policies). Sure, banners, buttons, and stickers can promote how important your Customers are; but there are no-kidding tangible things that you can do to drive Customer-centricity into your company's culture. Take it from a cold-hearted military analyst!

As I wrap up Part II of this book, ideally that cold-hearted military (or perhaps an emotionless alien?) approach has at least come some way toward offering up a correction to the shortcomings of the traditional CX approach I outlined in Part I.

But we're not finished. This framework I just outlined is simply an idea. To make it real, we need to put moving parts in place. In Part III, we'll explore the next steps in making that happen. We'll fill in the blanks and put faces into spaces.

PART III: PUTTING IT INTO ACTION

It's said that personnel is policy. The preceding framework *will* work, but you need to put in place an entire structure within your company to execute on anything. Without *boots on the ground*, even the most clever and groundbreaking ideas won't come to fruition.

Emotionless aliens and cold-hearted military analysts agree with Picasso and Emerson: You have to take *action* to make things happen.

In this final part of the book, I'll share with you some ways to structurally build out and staff your Office of the Customer and hire a Chief Customer Officer. I'll also offer some final thoughts on how to ensure success in your own CX journey.

CHAPTER 7: OFFICE OF THE CUSTOMER

Words on a page can be powerful, but not nearly as much as words put into action. The framework I described in Part II is one I've implemented myself, and it generally works well. Your mileage may vary, of course, but you can't edit a blank page, so it's a place to start nonetheless.

That said, though, it's surely not going to amount to much if you don't *do* something with it. In this chapter I'll show you what the functions within the Office of the Customer will accomplish and who you'll need to staff this vital department.

We'll get to the leadership, in the "Chief Customer Officer," in Chapter 8, but what follows here is a description of the team he or she will lead. As you'd expect, it implements the three-part framework. What follows are the three organizations within the Office of the Customer: the Insights, Process Engineering, and CX Culture teams. As a note to the reader, your company may not need to hire dozens of analysts for your Insights organization or fifty Black Belts for Process Engineering. While I'll be using terms like *Division* and *Director* for the purpose of simplicity, this entire framework is scalable; and no matter the size of your company (or these parts of it), the Office of the Customer should manage and execute these roles and responsibilities.

Insights Division

Customer Experience work starts with the Voice of the Customer. Unfortunately, in some organizations, that's also where it ends. But if you're reading this book, it's because you feel it's important to have other moving parts, which we'll get to shortly. But yes, the first of these is Customer Insights.

The key outcome of the Insights Division is actionable *information*. Your Director of Insights should have that as his or her mission: delivering direction regarding the gaps between your Brand Promise and what your Customers are experiencing when they interact with your brand. Basically, answer this question: How are we missing the mark when it comes to Brand Alignment?

Now, as I outlined in Chapter 4, there's more to VoC than just surveys: There are interviews, social media listening, curating online reviews, market analysis, Customer panels, and, of course, walking in the Customers' shoes.

An entire team within the division may be focused on the surveys. Your surveys should be dynamic and shift when new insights point you in new directions. The perfect survey is a moving target as the results should inform further questions to ask in the future. When you derive useful insights from the questions you're asking, they'll spark further questions, not only to more precisely understand what's going on but to understand other, peripheral issues that may be associated with what you learned first. It's not that you'll simply continue adding questions indefinitely (surveys should be kept as brief as possible); it's that insight begets insight by way of piquing your own curiosity. The more you know, the more you *want* to know. It gets to be a full-time job.

What's more, the insights will inspire new initiatives as you move to close the gaps you've identified. That, in turn, will require tracking results of these endeavors, and, of course, what your Customers have to say about your efforts. Your survey maintenance will be constantly evolving. Simply keeping up with them will take a lot of work if you're doing it right.

That doesn't even take into account all those *other* sources of insights. Conducting interviews, recruiting and engaging with secret shoppers, working with focus groups, and, of course, walking in the Customers' shoes, takes a *lot* of work. Part of the team will juggle this work with a lot of balls in the air while keeping all these events on track.

Additionally, the Insights effort requires a team to do the analytics in order to turn the products of this work into actionable insights. You'll need extremely sharp and similarly curious business analysts, database administrators (there's a *lot* of data!), and people who are smart with visualization and building stories from numbers. This analytical super team will be responsible for turning the data that comes from all the sources you're leveraging for the Insights effort into something that makes sense and points the way definitively toward improvement.

Process Engineering Division

The information from your Insights Division will land on the desk of your Director of Process Engineering. What's nice about this division is that it's been done tons of times at companies of various sizes, across all industries, and around the world. Here is where the work gets done, guided by those insights. It's ironic that, while this is the most-often missed part of an overarching impactful CX function within a company, it's also the one that most frequently *already exists* somewhere in its own right in so many companies. You may already have a PE Division in your company. Now, let's give it a new mission!

As I mentioned in Chapter 5, Process Engineering has lots of flavors and even goes by many names from company to company. Some places call it the Business Process Management (BPM) Department, some call it BPI—swapping out "Improvement" for "Management," but it's the same function. Some call it CPI, making another switch, "Continuous" for "Business." It's also basically the same thing. An observer could be excused for simply considering it alphabet soup. The bottom line, though, is that it doesn't really matter what it's called (I happen to prefer "Process Engineering"), so long as it's clear what it *does* and what it's responsible for.

Typically, whatever its name, the PE Division is charged with improving processes and systems with the ultimate goal of improving the bottom line through resource savings. These savings are realized by more efficient ways of working and resource use that result in less waste and less error in processes. Normally, this division's day-to-day work will include mentoring and coaching the leaders of these projects as well as outreach, awareness, and training in skills like Lean, Six Sigma, Kaizen, and other such disciplines. Responsibility for and authority over the actual projects are usually given to process *owners* from within the organizations in which they are normally driven. These process owners improve their *own* processes by the practice of these PE skills under the tutelage of the Black Belts from the PE organization.

While it *does* happen, rarely does someone from the PE Division oversee (and have responsibility for and authority over) the actual *initiatives* that are being implemented and process improvement projects as they're in flight. In some cases, they'll take a more active role in particular projects, such as when they're broad enough to span across several parts of the company or when the expected impact or visibility of a project or its unique needs require a more seasoned practitioner. Usually, practitioners at this heightened level of expertise (such as Master Black Belts) work within the PE Division anyway as that's where their skills are best put to use. In those situations, that expert may actually "*run*" a project and have direct responsibility, perhaps even over a matrixed team of people from different organizations.

There are a few major ways the PE Division should approach its work differently when it's part of a CX organization:

First of all, the entire charter is slightly tweaked in that the *purpose* of—and therefore the prioritization among—the projects it executes is different. Rather than resource use (and cost savings and such) as the main goal and metric, in this dynamic the driving factor is your Brand Alignment. The PE Division is *not* searching, simply for the biggest financial "bang for the buck" in choosing which projects to pursue or measuring their success when completed; rather, it's looking for the biggest gaps in your Brand Alignment and for ways to improve *that*. Now, as I've mentioned before, yes, two things can be true. And yes, improving processes and systems that drive poor CX likely will *also* relieve inefficiencies that will *also* save you money. And as I mentioned earlier in the book, when you prioritize based on CX, you can add to those savings the additional *revenue* that will come from having more satisfied Customers and greater word-of-mouth marketing. So, it's a good thing, and we don't really *have* to choose.

That said, though, this leads to another difference in this PE shop: As your CCO is hiring Green Belts, Black Belts, and Master Black Belts to carry out this PE mission, search for those with that skill set who are *also* Customer-focused. It's sad but true that a lot of Process Engineers get so caught up in improving processes and developing efficiencies (it can be a lot of fun if you're into that sort of nerdy thing) that they don't seem to care enough about end Customers and usually are only looking for ways to save resources and money. I've been there, I know. PE is an incredibly in-demand skill and lots of companies are looking for people who are good at it to drive their bottom line. That's not a bad appetite to have, and there are definitely places for it. But when you find practitioners who also appreciate the perspective of doing it to better align *Customers' experiences*, you've struck gold. The very nature of your PE Division will be different when you select your process engineers this way.

Another huge difference between this PE Division and your typical one? The practitioners will all be *leading* projects. You should read that as "responsible for" and "with authority to carry out." As I have mentioned, typically (but, granted, not always), the main day-to-day work of the Black Belts and Green Belts within your PE Division or team is mentorship. They're not as much responsible for the oversight of and outcomes from the various PE endeavors throughout the company, as they play in an advisory position—helping out as needed and offering guidance to process owners who work on *their own* improvement projects. As part of a PE Division within your CX organization, rather, they'll be heading up these projects, leading the teams, taking responsibility for outcomes, and directing activities. That's not always a typical role for a Black Belt and sometimes not even for Master Black Belts, whose main jobs are more *guru*ish in nature. The main reason for a focus like this is that nearly all the projects you'll need to initiate from an enterprise-wide CX perspective will span across multiple silos and organizations within the company.

To drive the desired impact, someone from *outside* these organizations should be held responsible for the outcome of the effort. There is no time or place for squabbles over authority and ownership. Someone representing the *Customer* should be in charge so as to avoid turf battles that only slow down the improvement process. I'll have more to say about this in the next chapter, but suffice it to say that if you want results you've got to put someone in charge with no skin in the game. A stand-alone PE Division working on behalf of the CX organization is just the place to find somebody without a vested interest in "the way we've always done it" to make the sort of changes you're seeking. So put the responsibility—and the authority—where it belongs: in the hands of the change-makers.

One way that this design is similar to more traditional PE shops is the previously mentioned dedication to mentoring, outreach, and training. Now, while I emphasize the importance of putting your PE practitioners in charge of the projects, it's still an awesome force multiplier to have a company full of curious and energetic process improvement advocates. Process Engineers will also tell you that an important part of their own professional development is just that sort of mentoring and coaching of others on the practice. Even though they'll spend more time *leading* projects than they would in a traditional PE setting, they'll still be itching (at least the good ones will) to get in front of a classroom and throw tennis balls around all day, teaching about the glories of Process Engineering. So, by all means, make sure they're also out there championing the practice and educating your whole team on how powerful it is to constantly be looking for ways to do what you do better.

Building that culture will go a long way toward building out the talent you need to knock out even better and bigger process improvements on behalf of your Customers. It's great to have a cadre of experts, but it's even *more* powerful to leverage that and drive enthusiasm and expertise throughout your entire company. More is better for sure in this case.

But that's obviously not the end to your culture work. And that's where the next part comes in.

CX Culture Division

The CX Culture Division has a complex mission. On one hand, it can easily be dismissed as the "feel-good" part of the organization. From that perspective, it could be argued (in large part, understandably) that it's not even needed. After all, you can always recruit a couple people who have a few minutes of time on their hands to hang the banners around the office. Sure, if outreach and messaging is all that's required, it may even be possible to create a volunteer committee of folks from across the organization and give them a moderate budget of petty cash to do everything from designing and ordering T-shirts and swag with inspirational Customer-centric mottos and logos to putting on rallies and other outreach events. That committee can also set up celebrations for CX day and even launch a few other awareness-focused initiatives that they come up with on their own (sponsored, of course, by the Chief Customer Officer). If that's all your CX Culture is, that's all it'd take.

But there's so much more to it than that, if it's *really* intended to make an impact.

Recall from Chapter 6, the three parts of CX culture: The Three E's. The messaging and internal marketing work that's usually most visible (and tragically most-often mistaken for an *actual* holistic "program") falls under the Encouragement banner. While Encouragement entails *much* more than simply these displays and messages—don't forget how important it is for the entire leadership team to *walk the talk*—even successful and robust Encouragement is really only a *part* of the charter for the CX Culture team. Don't forget the other two Es: Enablement and Empowerment.

As I pointed out in that chapter, you should see a parallel between the work of the overall CX organization (listening to and acting on your Customers' inputs) and the microcosm—more *inwardly* focused—of that dynamic in the CX Culture Division. To wit, there should be an active and energetic *listening* apparatus as well as a team dedicated to *acting* on what's heard. The difference here is that the target of the insights is the *employees* instead of the Customers. Within the CX Culture Division, there is a responsibility to take the pulse of the employees to learn from them what they're missing in order to do the job of advancing your Brand Promise. This would bring to light shortcomings of Enablement (they don't have the proper *tools*), Empowerment (the rules don't allow them the authority to best *use* the tools), or both. Think of it as a mini-Insights team—but more like a VoE team—working with a PE team taking action on what the employees say is needed.

Now, there may not be a need for an entire PE team (staffed with PMs, PEs, and the like) to make this happen. It may simply be coordination and active involvement with the *actual* CX PE Division, which should be easy since they all report up through the CCO. Basically, it's making sure that, in the overall prioritization and execution of CX PE efforts, the employees' perspective is also taken into account—not to replace or otherwise go *before* the desires of the Customers and not on the same level of importance of the Customers, but it should add some valuable perspective.

We have to keep in mind that the Customers come *first*. Yes, it's true that *employee* experience plays a *huge* role in the outcome of CX efforts, but understand that they (the employees) are *not* the focus in the end. That's not to take anything away from the fact that employees who interact regularly with the Customers bring some of the best insights to the effort. Quite the opposite, in fact. They know what's aching your Customers because they're working with them every day. They also have unique and valuable insights into what can be done to make their job (of helping the Customers achieve *their* goals, lest we forget) more productive from the Customers' perspective. For that matter, they're the bridge of experience between what your Customers are going through, and what your internal processes are.

But there's a balance between supporting your employees in ways that make their job of delivering your Brand Promise to your Customers easier and doing right by your employees simply because it's the right thing to do for your people. With that proper focus (the Customers), it becomes a virtuous cycle of mutual respect and shared purpose. Without it, it's a self-serving—and eventually, self-devouring—cycle of mistaking the entire reason your company is in business.

This is a touchy subject, and I've been in forums where some CX professionals have stated with great frankness and certainty that they consider their *employees* to be their Customers. The risks of taking that approach far outweigh the temporary rush of good feelings—and even genuine good will—it'll deliver around the office. It won't take long before the guiding star of delivering your Brand Promise to your Customers is shadowed by conflicting and confusing messages from leadership when what it takes to satisfy these two constituencies doesn't align (and believe me, those instances *will* occur). Bottom line here: Considerably weigh employee insights about how to better align your Customers' experiences with your Brand Promise (especially from employees on the front-lines); work toward Enabling and Empowering these team members to best serve your Customers. But don't mistake your employees *for* your Customers.

This is the charter of your CX Culture Division. It should be led by a dynamic, people-centric director who understands CX as a profession and has a good grasp of team dynamics and a bit of marketing experience, as internal messaging plays such an important role. In some dynamics, this can be done, in fact, with a dual-hatted leader from the HR organization—someone already working in the overall corporate culture space. That's not a bad idea as this, the CX part of the culture work, needs to be integrated with and certainly not in conflict with the overall work on your enterprise cultural efforts. For that matter, though, if you're inclined to house this entire function within the CX organization (which I recommend), filling this position with a rising star within your HR department can be a great career advancement for the right candidate and can benefit the position by bringing the right skillset to the job.

As I stated previously, your mileage may vary when it comes to the applicability of my specific framework (with Insights, PE, and CX Culture as segments). And again, if yours is a smaller, leaner company, you won't need to go on a hiring binge in order to find success. As such, your Office of the Customer may or may not necessarily *look* the same. These three moving parts, however, do need leadership, differentiation, and accountability. If you choose a different framework (or alter or scale this one), the design of your Office of the Customer will likely look different.

One thing is for sure though: You *need* an Office of the Customer. I've heard plenty of people say that, "CX is *everybody's* job." While it's definitely great to have the entire enterprise on board with your CX efforts, engineers will still have to engineer, sales will still have to sell, and finance will still have to tell everybody what they can and cannot afford to do. *Somebody* has to direct and focus the CX efforts in your organization. *Someone* has to provide the vision and strategy of your Customer-centric efforts and to lead the way and prioritize the CX endeavors. Frame it any way you like, but you'll still need a staff to coordinate the work.

And naturally, you'll need some*one* to lead that staff. In the next chapter, we'll explore the job of the Chief Customer Officer and what it takes to be a great CCO.

CHAPTER 8: THE CHIEF CUSTOMER OFFICER

It's never a trivial matter to add a new member to your leadership team. Hiring a Chief Customer Officer can be even more consequential. As I wrote earlier, personnel is policy: A mistake in hiring your Chief Customer Officer can have pretty disastrous effects, mostly because the role is still not very widely seen. It's fair to say that many organizations will get only one bite out of this apple since initial failure can lead to cynicism and very slim odds at a second chance. So, it'll be important to know not only *what* the roles and responsibilities of your CCO will be but also *who* will make a good candidate.

First, I'll walk through a high-level breakdown of the CCO's role, and analogously we'll see that it's not really all that alien (pun intended) from what you already see when you look around your C-Suite.

Then we'll look at what characteristics are most valuable in the selection of the individual to fill this important position. Now, I wouldn't deign to suggest to a CEO and assembled leadership team that I'm an expert in hiring. Nor would I recommend *replacing* any cultural and pre-existing qualifications in place for joining your C-Suite. Having been an executive team member myself, I am aware and respectful of the importance of cultural and interpersonal fit among the leadership team.

My recommendations here are meant as an *adjunct* to whatever your usual criteria are in looking for leaders at this level of your organization; what specifically applies to *this* executive. That said, where they diverge may be an opportunity for reflection wherever you end up in the final determination of your hiring process.

CCO Functional Roles

It may be the rarity of the role, but at first, a lot of business leaders wonder what a Chief Customer Officer even *is*. While some of the responsibilities are new—or at least new to *think about* at this level or in this way—the theory and day-to-day are pretty easy to understand in relation to things that already exist in most corporate structures. I break the job functions of a CCO down to "operational" and "representative" responsibilities. Frankly, when you look at it that way, it's not really that different from any of the new CCO's peers on the leadership team.

Let's take the CFO, for example. Now, your company may also have a Controller, Treasurer, and other sundry "money people" doing some financial things, but for simplicity's sake, let's say you have a CFO as practically your Chief All-Things-Money-Related Officer. As such, on the operational side, the Chief Finance Officer is responsible for a great number of things. A couple big ones, for example: one, that everything that's owed to the company is collected and accounted for; and two, that everything the company owes to others is likewise remitted and accounted for.

The CFO oversees a pretty complicated and sprawling team of professionals that sends out payments to suppliers, oversees proper payroll execution, and ensures that quarterly tax payments are funded and sent out. They're the folks approving advertising budgets, reviewing warehousing contracts for cost, and, of course, keeping an eye on those travel expenses. There's also the responsibility for ensuring proper invoicing to Customers, channel partners, and licensees and vendors, and following up with collections and accounts receivable. That's an entire *operation* to take care of, and your CFO is responsible for making all those things—plus so much more—happen.

Similarly, your Chief Customer Officer has responsibility and authority for all the things I described in the previous chapter: *running* the Office of the Customer. Your CCO runs the Insights, PE, and CX Culture programs. As I noted earlier, these are actual heavy lifts. There's a *lot* involved in running each of these programs, and the enterprise-wide nature of their execution and impact requires someone at the helm, steering that ship and running that show.

Now, back to the CFO, the other part of his or her job is a representative one. As a member of the leadership team, your CFO brings the important perspective of finance to choices that are made as a group. Whenever an issue arises that requires a leadership decision, inevitably one of the considerations is the cost/benefit analysis. How much will it cost to switch from one supplier to another? What would be the financial impact of opening up a new branch in Seattle? What should we expect as a return on launching a Spanish language version of our product—how big is that segment and what's the *Total Addressable Market* there? These sorts of insights require financial expertise, and it's important to have someone at the table representing this concern as decisions are being made.

Again, your CCO will play an analogous role: one representing the constituency of the Customer. If, for example, the head of your product group decides to re-engineer a certain part of your product, it will be the Chief Customer Officer's responsibility to evaluate the impact of that change on the *Customer*, just as the head of Supply Chain will have to weigh in on the changes to logistics of acquiring new sub-components for the change and the COO will concern himself or herself with whether re-tooling will be required in the manufacturing facility. All of these leaders will have to come together to make a decision that will work based on all the moving parts. Thanks to your CCO, the Customer will have a seat at the table as well.

It's worth noting, and here seems an appropriate place, by the way, to mention a couple reasons you need an Office of the Customer led by a Chief Customer Officer in the first place. One of the typical topics of small talk at any gathering of CX professionals is, Where is the CX organization located in your corporate structure? That dovetails well with this common concern from many business leaders: Why do I need this to be at the C-Suite level? Consider some thoughts on this:

I'm aware that some companies put the CX organization within Customer Service, Customer Support, or Customer Success. The problem with that? CX is an enterprise-wide organization that's intended to impact and improve processes, operations, and policies throughout your *entire* company. Putting it within the support, service, or success groups means it'll have only a narrow focus. Someone from CS (whichever "S" that stands for) won't be able to go into the operations organization or the engineering group and direct that things change on behalf of the Customers. While I'm certain that the leaders of these organizations are fully behind the drive toward Customer-centricity, having someone show up at their door from, for example, the Customer Service Division and explaining what needs to change there is not likely to end well. Believe me, I've been there.

But what about, say, Marketing or Sales? They're both dedicated to Customers, right? Surely they are, and are more than likely incredibly well-connected with the Customers and their desires too. So, that's great; would that *all* organizations within the company were so laser-focused on the Customers. But in fact, that's part of the issue: Sales and Marketing are both focused *outwardly* in their perspective as well as their purview.

The job of Marketing is to present the Brand Promise to the Customer or potential Customer. The job of Sales is to close the deal with the Customer or potential Customer. The job of CX, on the other hand, is to turn *internally*, based on what the Customers are experiencing, and adjust what we do *ourselves* as a company so as to better align with our Brand Promise. Marketing and Sales both are responsive to changes in Customers' desires and wants, to be sure. They're also sensitive to instances of the brand not living up to its promise. But the changes they make in response on these occasions are more toward their own tactics (of either marketing or selling), and they're certainly *not* expected to change the very nature of the company's overall processes, policies, systems, and procedures as a result. In a failure to meet the Brand Promise, for example, Sales and Marketing would endeavor to put the best face on the circumstances. They wouldn't be expected to *fix* the systemic issues at the root of the problem itself. That's CX's job.

Finally—and this goes for all potential other *homes* for CX within the organization—I invite you to re-read the previous chapter. Insights, PE, and CX Culture each are (if done right) huge enterprise-wide activities. While I have no doubt that your CMO, Head of Customer Support, and even COO are well-accomplished, dedicated, vigorous, and competent members of your leadership team, they have a long list of responsibilities already. Do you think any of them would want to add to that not just the whole Customer Insights program but also every end-to-end process improvement effort needed to *improve* the CX across the entire company? If done right, the job of CX is a

C-Suite level responsibility and authority.

CCO Characteristics

So, you know what your CCO will be called upon to do. But, who's right for that job? Well, as I've mentioned, I'm not an HR guru and I don't think you should replace your established approach to filling out your C-Suite and leadership team. But what follows are four very important character traits of a good CCO. These, when added to your usual requirements for joining your leadership, will ensure that you have a great leader who will make a tremendously positive impact on your business.

The first characteristic vital to a good Chief Customer Officer is *Curiosity*. Now, that's a bit of a freebie, as curiosity is valuable in *any* position. I always hire for curiosity and always have at any level of responsibility or within any organization. I don't allow it to overshadow competence and good character, but I've never hired anybody who I didn't at least think had a thirst for learning more and experiencing new things.

It's even more important when hiring someone into a CX role (again, even if it's not the top of the organization) because there's so much ambiguity in what the CX professional encounters every day. Those who need structure and require a systematic way of doing everything are awesome in certain roles; but those who can innovate thanks to a thirst and desire to learn things are more likely to take a step out of your corporate environment to better understand what it's like to be a *Customer* of yours.

A Process Engineer who worked for me used a saying that I stole from him and that I still use all the time: We need to take off our corporate hats and put on our Customer hats. That sentiment and approach is born out of a curiosity that drives someone to think differently and yearn for alternative points of view. Even in the field of CX, it amazes me how many folks lack the curiosity to consider new perspectives and different ways of operating (c.f., the silly fights people have over NPS). Some of the suggestions in this very book will drive some of them mad. Here, we're in a profession that implores other business leaders to see things differently and take a different perspective (that of our Customers), and yet so many of us refuse to think outside the box of established ways of approaching CX. Don't just rely on a professional CX certification and consider you've got the right new Chief Customer Officer. Test your candidate's curiosity, and see how he or she thinks. You'll thank yourself for doing so, as the new member of your leadership will come in and challenge your team in ways that will pay dividends.

The second characteristic for a successful CCO is an *Analytical Mind*. Now, I'm a statistician and a professor of stats myself. I wouldn't say I'm the *best* analyst, but I can surely hold my own. You don't need to hire someone with that pedigree to be your Chief Customer Officer. But it *has* to be someone not only comfortable with stats and math but who understands analytics well enough to tell stories with numbers.

I had a boss (who's still a mentor) who holds a BA in literature but who nonetheless runs circles around me analytically, and she always has. What's more, this business leader is a pro at simplifying complicated mathematical thoughts into accessible and applicable stories. *That's* analytical ability in my book: self-taught, relatable, practical, and down-to-earth. Your CCO will likely be what I call an analyst *whisperer*, often "translating" the work done by the analytical shop within your Insights Division into C-Suite and boardroom pictures that make sense to everybody. It's not handwaving or prevaricating; it's making sense of numbers. And it doesn't take a statistician. But it *does* take some analytical acumen.

Another important characteristic of your CCO is *Diversity*. I don't mean this the way we've come to know the term. This isn't about everybody on your leadership team not *looking* alike, but it's about your team not all *thinking* alike. As much trouble as I get into in CX circles for some of my unorthodox approaches and philosophies, I never get as much pushback from business leaders as when I recommend to them that they invite into the inner sanctum of their leadership teams someone not only from outside their organization but from outside their *industry*.

We all carry baggage and preconceptions, and that's inevitable. Even the most squared-away personality and self-aware leader (aren't they *all* supposed to be self-aware?) is the product of his or her experiences. The role of CCO is unique in that, *not* having too much experience in an industry can actually *benefit* the performance of the job. If you're the CEO of a hospital, you definitely want a surgeon to be the Chief of Surgery. You don't want someone without any sales experience to head up your sales division. Your CIO had better know his or her way around a data center (well, or the *cloud* these days). And it's true, not *everybody* knows CX as a profession.

My earlier comment to not *rely* simply on a CX certification isn't meant to denigrate it as a field or put no stock in the knowledge of how to do this *sort* of job. But within your industry (the things you sell or the services you provide), I guarantee there are systemic ways you do things. Think of the conferences you attend, the vendors who supply you as well as your competitors, and the conversations you have with your peers. There are built-in things within your industry that are *de rigueur* and pass through your ecosystem like water around fish. These are *exactly* the sorts of things that your Chief Customer Officer and the Office of the Customer are there to smash through. It's in the commonalities within your industry that you'll find the opportunities to stand apart.

When your competition is making excuses because *well, that's the way it goes in this sort of business*, a CCO, representing your *Customer* will ask, "Why should that be the case?" Ideally, he or she isn't doing so simply to be clever or trite—but with that voice at the table, you can start to view things from the perspective of the impacts they have on your Customers instead of those of people who have never known anything different. So, bluntly, find a Chief Customer Officer who knows your industry as a *Customer*, not as a player in it.

Finally, and hopefully not too surprisingly, you need a CCO who's *Diplomatic*. This person is going to be that iconoclast or little boy from *The Emperor's New Clothes*, upending industry standards in how you approach your work. Your Chief Customer Officer will start, day one, as someone without blinders or scales on his or her eyes. This new team member will take a fresh look at how you interact with your Customers, curious to learn where you're missing the mark with your Brand Promise. Internally—again, if you're doing it right—you'll give this person the authority to knock on the door of any peer on the leadership team, sit down, and have a heart-to-heart about how "the way we do business needs to change." Naturally, a lot of the improvement efforts will entail working across the different organizations within your company.

This sort of matrixed work takes well-seasoned and well-crafted interpersonal skills. But there may even be times when the improvement needs to take place within only *one* organization. This takes even *more* delicacy as it's one thing to be the arbitrator between competing silos, all at least nominally focused on a shared goal of driving Brand Alignment. It's even harder to let someone into your metaphorical kitchen and watch as that person fiddles around with your stove. I've often joked that, as powerful as the CFO is, it's a great sign of the maturity of a company's CX efforts if the Chief Customer Officer can look across the table at the CFO and explain, "Well, our VoC analysis shows that the number one defect in meeting our Brand Promise of being an easy-to-work-with brand lies in our billing process. With whom from your organization should our Black Belts work to address this?" Yes, diplomacy is vital.

So, your CCO needs to be *Curious, Analytical, Different,* and *Diplomatic.* Piece of cake!

Adding a new member to your leadership team (or replacing one) is a non-trivial endeavor. Not only is it a lot of *work* looking for and placing the right person, it comes with a lot of stress and import. What's more, if you follow my advice here, you'll likely be bringing in someone quite unfamiliar to his or her new peers. Making such a move without knowing the person is surely somewhat risky. But, as the Latin proverb says, *fortis Fortuna adiuvat*, or, "Fortune favors the bold." Remember, CX is a way of differentiating yourself and your brand. It requires boldness to stand by your Brand Promise and make changes where necessary in what you *do* so that you can *be* what you say you *are* to your Customers.

Seek out someone with that shared boldness, give him or her the room to do the job, and I guarantee you'll match your words to deeds in no time.

CHAPTER 9: SOME PARTING THOUGHTS FOR THE CEO

Initiating a CX journey, hiring a CCO, and staffing an Office of the Customer is not a set-it-and-forget-it endeavor. You must consider some things *before* you strike off on this course of action and, as you get going, I've put together some caveats to keep mind so you don't run off the rails.

There are also a few random extra thoughts I figured would be helpful to leaders who are interested in taking this path.

Don't Abandon Your CCO

Customer Experience guru Jeanne Bliss often says the CX leader is most responsible for stitching between silos. Not shy about mixing metaphors, she even refers to the person filling the role as "Human Duct Tape" (also the title to her fantastic podcast, which I recommend). It's true (as I mentioned in the last chapter) that diplomacy is a very valuable characteristic of a successful CCO. It's also important—as the CEO specifically and more broadly as the existing executive leadership team as a whole—to understand the role everybody else plays in the CX efforts.

Of course, CX as an endeavor takes support and enthusiasm from the top. Naturally, also it's vital that the new Chief Customer Officer walks into a situation where he or she feels supported and whose mission is accepted by the rest of the leadership team. I've seen CX professionals hired into leadership positions, given a charter to improve CX, allowed to hire a staff and afforded carte blanche over the CX infrastructure, yet fail because the expected impact and methods of achieving it weren't clearly agreed upon and articulated beforehand. Moreover, it's usually because the actual *role* isn't agreed upon before starting.

It's a common mistake to go out and hire a diplomatic team player with a knack for getting people on board and rallying around an important idea like CX and call it a day. That's a mistake because for a CX initiative to take hold and succeed, everybody else in the leadership team needs to feel comfortable with someone else, frankly, *messing around* with their operations. That's a huge ask, especially if it's someone *new* to the leadership team (if you're following my advice to hire someone from outside of your industry).

As the CEO, you can ensure the success of your new CX organization by clarifying for the entire leadership team that the Chief Customer Officer is *not* simply going to be "the new survey guy" or "that lady who's going to get us all on board with being more Customer-centric." This is a serious position, and it comes with a serious charter to *change the way your business does business* in large and small ways to drive alignment between your Brand Promise and your Customers' experiences. I've spoken with *lots* of CX leaders who, a few months into the job of CCO, are frustrated by the recalcitrance of their leadership peers to allow change to take place. Every leadership team experiences turf battles and personality conflicts (don't pretend that's not the case). And yes, I'll reiterate, your CCO needs to be hired in part based on his or her skills at getting along and playing nice with others. But if you're relying *just* on that personality to grease the gears of improvement, you're doing yourself, your new CCO, and your entire organization a disservice.

Before you even begin looking for a new Chief Customer Officer, it's vital that you explain to the entire leadership team (and get their buy-in) the purpose of—and what to expect from—a new CX function. Each of your C-Suite members represents an organization within your company that impacts the Customers' experiences. As such, each one of them will potentially be in the crosshairs of improvement efforts. As such, each will possibly face the day when your new CCO comes knocking, asking questions about, and proposing changes to, his or her processes. You as the CEO can go a long way in making those interactions more productive and positive if you've set this expectation before you even start your search.

For that matter, you'll likely be enlisting other members of the leadership team to help find, or at least vet the candidates, for your CCO role. *Before* they do so is an excellent time to let them know that the person they're interviewing as a potential future peer is also going to be someone they'll have to feel comfortable with futzing around in their business. It definitely would change my approach, and questions I'd ask, if I knew that was a future possibility.

Plus, by making it clear that this new hire is going to have the authority to make changes across the *entire enterprise*, it oughtn't come as a surprise when he or she asserts that authority. This surely won't guarantee no friction whatsoever—you can never do that. But it's one thing to get irked that "the new guy" is monkeying with your systems; it's another thing altogether when that comes as a shock to you out of the blue because proper expectations weren't set in the first place.

So, the bottom line here is simple: Don't rely *just* on the great personality of your new CCO. Start laying the groundwork and setting the expectations *before* you get started in your search. And along your journey and after you've filled the position, don't abandon your new Chief Customer Officer.

About That "Misalignment"

Another important topic to address in this hodgepodge section of the book goes back to something I wrote earlier: I mentioned that, when faced with the "ROI question" of CX, I turn it around on business leaders and instead ask them if they believe that better alignment between their Brand Promise and what their Customers experience when they interact with their brand would produce better business results. And yes, everybody always answers in the affirmative.

But there's a corollary to that question: What if it *doesn't*? It's similar to what Bob, our friend who ran that Betamax VCR repair shop had to face. Sometimes, the market simply doesn't have a place for your Brand Promise. Perhaps nobody wants a *luxury* brand of the widgets you make because they've become so commoditized that everybody wants to simply go to the store and buy a dozen of them off the shelf and not even bother knowing whose brand it is. Nobody wants that exquisite experience when they're buying what you're selling. Or perhaps the technology of your product is esoteric and novel enough still that the market isn't ready for a *discount* brand just yet. Customers would consider it a *knockoff* and blanch at the prospect of owning a lesser brand (whether that estimation of your product is fair or not). Or like Bob, maybe there's literally just no longer a *need* for it.

And that's the problem with using ROI as an arguing point for "doing CX." If a CX practitioner comes into a company, convinces leadership that they should "do CX" and as a result, they'll reap untold monetary rewards for their dedication to the Customer, but then doesn't deliver, it'll be easy for that company do decide, "Well, *that* was a bust! I'd say we're done with CX."

Not only does that break my heart as a true believer in CX, it's also a huge wasted opportunity. Since the goal there was never Brand Alignment, the brand itself is never brought into question if things go pear-shaped. On the other hand, if the purpose of CX from the start was Brand Alignment, the conversation about the viability of your Brand Promise can (and likely will) happen.

Say, over the course of a year, your BAS goes through the roof from a baseline score of 20 all the way to 80, but your sales KPIs don't improve. Since CX will have (demonstrably) done its job of improving alignment between your Customers' experiences and your Brand Promise, you'll then be at liberty to question that very Brand Promise itself instead of scapegoating the entire practice of Customer Experience.

That conversation won't be comfortable or easy to have, probably. Those never are. But it won't be clouded—or worse, missed altogether—by finger-pointing and blame-shifting. The team can say, "Well, CX did its job. We've driven greater Brand Alignment. We're definitely living up to what we're promising, based on Customers' feedback. But people simply aren't buying what we're selling. Perhaps there's not a market for the niche we've so successfully established. Let's reflect on that and consider possible different approaches."

Alternatively, if ROI was the whole reason you "did CX" all along, the whole endeavor is going to seem like a sham and a waste of money. Tragically, that'll actually be the case.

So, here's the bottom line: Don't be so sure you've got the winning formula for your Brand Promise. CX can help drive that Brand Alignment, but if that alignment doesn't end up with tons of revenue and sales, something more fundamental may be going on. At least feel confident you've learned the right lesson.

Hire Fractional

Not all organizations will benefit from hiring a Chief Customer Officer. Some companies aren't quite there yet. A couple of buddies from college, building the next best new mousetrap in the garage of their Silicon Valley house, probably don't need a *lot* of things yet: COO, CFO, CHRO, etc. I'd certainly put the Chief Customer Officer in that category. For that matter, as I alluded to in Chapter 7, not every company is large enough to require a sprawling Office of the Customer with VPs, directors, and dozens of employees.

That *doesn't* mean such organizations don't need *CX*, per se. But just like with those other leadership roles, fortunately, a cadre of CX professionals out there can assist you wherever you are and to whatever degree you need it. I couldn't let this book close without mentioning the value of a Fractional Chief Customer Officer. I probably don't have to go on at great length describing *what* a Fractional CCO is as it's right up the same alley as all those others (CFO, CHRO, etc.) out there. The concept is the same: You bring one in on a *fractional* basis. He or she may even have another client or two, but the main job is to get you up and running on what will be your Office of the Customer (or rebuilding if you're looking to improve what you have), just like any other fractional officer would do.

One great benefit of hiring a Fractional CCO is that it almost guarantees a unique perspective. CX professionals who work fractionally are *much* more likely to be curious, diplomatic, and experienced in a wide range of industries. These folks have seen more and experienced more. Plus, of course, it's more likely they'll also fill the role of *outsider*, which can be valuable beyond measure, especially as you're just embarking upon your CX journey.

Consider that a possible engagement may work something like this (the timing can be different—and as previously mentioned, the scope may vary considerably—but the layout is usually along these lines):

- Quarter 1: Assessing, baselining Brand Alignment, building Customer Insights (VoC) programming, familiarizing with internal processes, starting CX culture efforts, and hiring mostly for the Insights team, but also some PE resources

- Quarter 2: Formalizing Insights program, hiring Insights lead, continuing to hire Process Engineers, hiring PE lead, engaging in Process Improvement efforts, expanding CX culture programs

- Quarter 3: Slowly ramping down Fractional work, standing up CX Culture team, recruiting and vetting of full-time CCO (Fractional CCO should play a role in this as well), then handing off to new CCO

The bottom line here? Consider starting off slowly with a Fractional Chief Customer Officer, ramping it up over the course of a year or so and then taking off with a full-time CCO once you've got the system up and running.

You're a business leader. Clearly, I don't have to tell you that you never know what could go wrong. Robert Burns may not have been the maven of business school, but we all learn plenty about the best laid plans of mice and men from our own experiences. For that matter, no less a poet than Mike Tyson is well known for his observation that, "everyone has a plan until they get punched in the mouth."

But that's not an excuse to lack direction and purpose, and nobody goes into battle without a plan. This book has presented one to you.

So, here we are: We've articulated several ways in which business leaders are doing CX wrong; we've identified why that is (an erroneous philosophy and approach); we've seen a framework built on an appropriate CX purpose; and finally, we've identified all the moving parts (and people!) that will need to be put into place.

We've now reached the moment of truth … and action.

As a drill instructor used to tell us when I was in the Air Force's Officer Training School, "There's nothing left to do but to do it."

I hope you've found this interesting and applicable. This is surely not the last word on CX, but I've read enough business books to recognize that there's a huge difference between a philosophical pronouncement and delivering results. With this book, I aimed to offer a way for CEOs and business leaders to *act and deliver* on the promise of Customer Experience as an operation: To bring alignment between your Brand Promise and what your Customers experience when they interact with your brand.

Now, go out there and do it!

Oh, and feel free to reach out if you need help. Or just to share your story.

ABOUT THE AUTHOR

 Lt. Col. Nicholas "Z" Zeisler is a CXPA Certified Customer Experience Professional, a Lean Six Sigma Black Belt, a Certified Scrum Master, and a recovering PMP. He's a former Fortune 100 CX executive, an independent consultant and a Fractional Chief Customer Officer. As a Reservist, he's an Assistant Professor at the US Air Force Academy where he teaches Statistics. Over 20 years of consulting, he's helped companies in industries as varied as energy, technology, insurance, government, healthcare, and non-profits with clients large and small. He's hosted dozens of webinars, keynoted conferences, and guested on countless podcasts sharing his message about the importance of having a purpose for CX and taking action to make it happen. He lives in Denver, Colorado, with his partner and their awesome dog. When not working, he spends summers at baseball games and winters skiing. You can reach him by following the nearby QR code or visiting zeislerconsulting.com.

Made in the USA
Middletown, DE
24 September 2021

48941309R00066